Where There Is No Name for Art

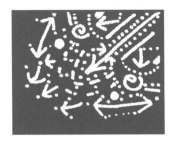

The publication of this book

was made possible in part by a grant from the Annenberg Foundation.

Art and Voices of the Children of Santa Clara San Ildefonso San Juan Pojoaque and Nambé Pueblos

"SYMBOLS OF MY CULTURE"
HEATHER DASHENO, AGE 12
COLORED PENCIL

Where There Is No Name for Art

THE ART OF TEWA PUEBLO CHILDREN

Text and photographs by
BRUCE HUCKO

SAR PRESS • SCHOOL OF AMERICAN RESEARCH • SANTA FE, NEW MEXICO

School of American Research Press
Post Office Box 2188
Santa Fe, New Mexico 87504

Director of Publications: Joan K. O'Donnell
Editor: Jo Ann Baldinger
Designer: Deborah Flynn Post
Printer: Sung In Printing Company

Distributed by the University of Washington Press

Cataloging-in-Publication Data:
Hucko, Bruce.
    Where there is no name for art : the art of Tewa pueblo children /
text and photographs by Bruce Hucko. --1st ed.
        p. cm.
    Includes index.
    ISBN 0-933452-44-6 (pbk.)
    1. Tewa children--Education--Art. 2. Tewa art. 3. Children's
art--Southwest, New. I. Title.
CURR E99.T35H83 1996
    704'.03974--dc20   96-12833
                                              CIP

Front cover: Mark Cata in front of the kiva at San Ildefonso (south side).
Back cover: KhaPovi Harvier.

Line art by Daniel Archuleta, Jackie Lopez, Lee Moquino, Angela Pacheco,
Christine Pacheco, Jerome Tafoya, and Jackie Tsosie.
Map design by Carol Cooperrider.

Printed and bound in South Korea.

Spellings of Tewa names and words were provided by Frances Harney,
co-contributor to the *Ohkay Ówmgeh Tewa Language Dictionary* (San Juan Pueblo
Bilingual Program, revised 1995–96), according to the dialect of San Juan
Pueblo. Spellings and pronunciation marks may differ from one pueblo to
another; those of San Juan are used in this text for consistency and have
been simplified for the ease of reading.

This book is dedicated to all the generations:

those of the past, who set the pace for us,

those of the present, who carry tradition on their shoulders,

and those of the future,

who can look back with pride

in the knowledge that they have endured.

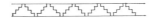

RAELENE GONZALES

Contents

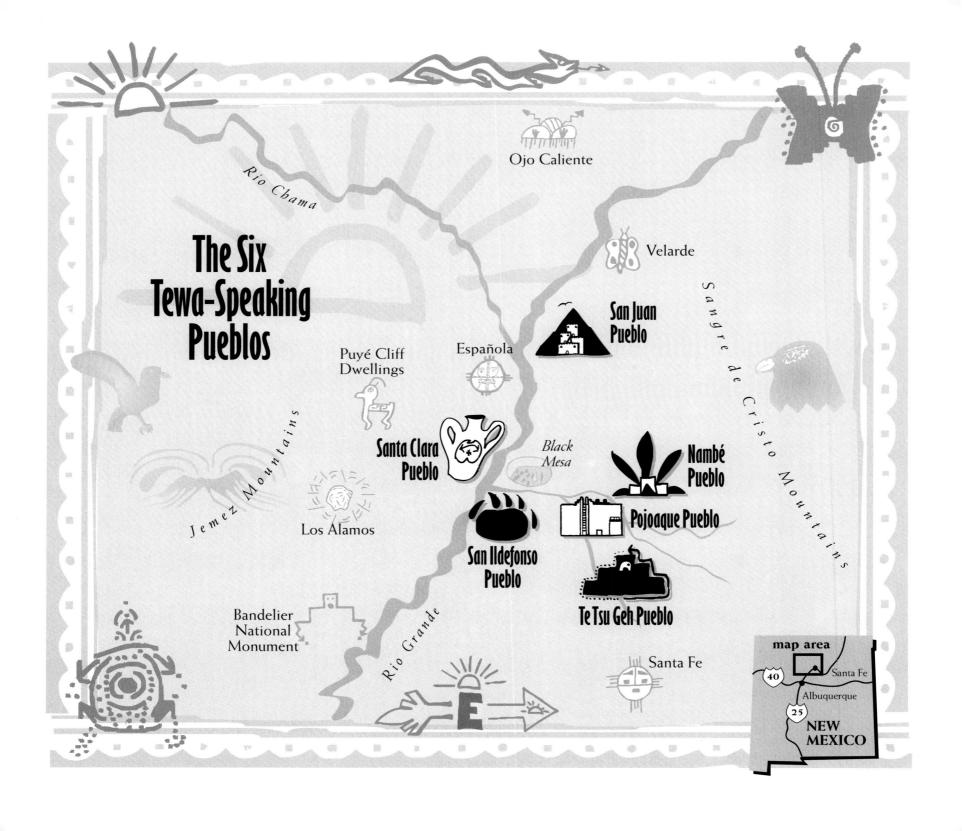

The Six Tewa-Speaking Pueblos

Ojo Caliente

Rio Chama

Velarde

San Juan Pueblo

Sangre de Cristo Mountains

Puyé Cliff Dwellings

Española

Santa Clara Pueblo

Black Mesa

Nambé Pueblo

Jemez Mountains

Los Alamos

Pojoaque Pueblo

San Ildefonso Pueblo

Te Tsu Geh Pueblo

Bandelier National Monument

Rio Grande

Santa Fe

E

map area

Santa Fe

40

Albuquerque

25

NEW MEXICO

"Art is important because it describes people's feelings and what they think about their people and their own ways. It describes their love for their cultures and people. Art is important to me because it expresses my feelings about my own culture."

—*Pauline Bourdon, age 12*

"RAINBOW PUEBLO"
ELIZA MORSE, AGE 11
WATERCOLOR

Don't Talk Too Much, Just Do Your Show!

AN INTRODUCTION

TEN-YEAR-OLD JACKIE TSOSIE sits at one end of a comfortable couch in the living room of her adobe home in Santa Clara Pueblo. After school, on weekends, or in the summer, Jackie can usually be found busy with one activity or another.

"I like to draw, play baseball, ride my bike, and read books," she says. Today Jackie is drawing birds and prairie dogs while she watches a TV movie called *Made in America*.

The television is surrounded by family photographs and paintings by famed artists and relatives such as Jackie's aunt, Helen Hardin, and great-aunt, Pablita Velarde. A colorful cottonwood drum belonging to her father stands next to the TV. Floor-to-ceiling shelves display the family's beautiful pottery in various stages of completion. Three of Jackie's own clay miniatures sit among them.

In the kitchen Jackie's mother and oldest sister are busy forming pottery. "They're playing with mud!" Jackie explains cheerfully. Her father is out, working at one of his several jobs: first-aid instructor, tribal judge, and emergency medical technician. Jackie's next older sister sits on another couch, watching television and folding clothes. Everyone is doing something—usually several "somethings" at once.

This is an everyday scene in the pueblos of the Rio Grande. Art is a rich and ancient tradition among Pueblo people, going back to the pictures their ancestors carved on stone and expressed nowadays most commonly in the creation of pottery. Contemporary Pueblo art is produced in a dynamic environment in which traditional forms overlap with modern media. This fusion is most evident in the art of Pueblo children. Through painting and drawing, a child's world of imagination and feeling becomes visible. It is that world that the children who made this book have chosen to share with you.

JACKIE TSOSIE

3

In their own language, Tewa Pueblo people have no word for art. Pottery, painting, embroidery, dance, and other "art" forms are not considered separate from life. On the contrary, art is seen as synonymous with work, thoughts, and expressions. The Pueblo world makes little or no distinction between baking bread, dancing, gardening, chopping wood, making pottery, or engaging in any other activity.

"I think that if there was no art there would be nothing on earth," says thirteen-year-old Jordan Harvier. "Like creation, everything, to me, is art." Among the Tewa Pueblo people of New Mexico, "art" springs from a place where all of life is interconnected—a place where there is no name for art.

It has been my good fortune during the past five years to serve as the "art coach" for the Pueblo day schools of San Juan, Santa Clara, and San Ildefonso. This book presents some of the delightful, vibrant art of the students at these schools.

Where There Is No Name for Art is more than a collection of pretty pictures, however. Among other things, it is a book about reciprocity. Through my work in the schools I have formed friendships with many of the children and their parents and have developed a deep respect for their communities. My students have given me so much—laughter, headaches, paint on my clothes. I hope this book gives back to the children, the parents, and the communities even a small portion of the pleasure I have received from them.

This book is also about continuity. For more than a thousand years the Pueblo people and their ancestors have made images on and about the land they call home. The images collected here are now part of that continuum of expression, a part that my students' own children and grandchildren will one day be able to enjoy.

This book is about community. Like any other community today, the Tewa villages face their share of social, environmental, economic, and cultural problems. There are divided homes, unemployment, economic disparity, alcoholism, drugs, violence, and the potential for cultural erosion due to the distractions of mainstream "American" culture. A range of social and economic forces are making it difficult for Pueblo communities to maintain their cultural integrity. The paramount intent of this project has been to celebrate the creative spirit and human wealth of these communities.

Community was also the guiding principle in determining how the text was assembled. All the voices you hear, all the images you see, come from the Tewa-speaking pueblos of northern New Mexico. In creating work about their lives and their communities, the children develop stronger connections to both. Every person quoted in this book, however, speaks as an individual, not as a representative of his or her pueblo. To do otherwise, the elders tell us, would be inappropriate and disrespectful.

This book is also about identity. I was curious about the children's perceptions of themselves. Who do they think they are? What is important to them? How do they see their world, and how does their art relate to that world? In addition, I conceived of this book as an opportunity for the children to take ownership of their work, to stand by their words, and to be able to say, at the end of this project, "See this book? I did it. I worked on it, and I am proud of it."

Finally, this book is about relationships. From the start we operated under the philosophy that working together would produce the best results. Children were involved in every step of the process. They created all the art. They were interviewed, they helped edit the text, and they contributed to book design, fundraising, and marketing. They also share in the profits. Each child whose work appears here receives an artist's fee from the publisher. In addition, a portion of my author's royalties will be donated to a Tewa Pueblo Children's Art Fund for the use of the children featured in the book, the Pueblo day schools, and community agencies providing art activities for children.

"WORKING WITH"

Because this book is by, and about, the Pueblo people's most valuable resource, the children, it demanded a different way of working. The record of publications about the Pueblos is a dismal one that includes repeated instances of betrayal, exploitation, and miscommunication. Understandably, the Pueblo people are cautious about what gets written about them.

From the start of this project, the notion of "working with" has been a guiding ethic. I had known most of the children, and some of their parents, for several years before I proposed the idea for a book. All of them expressed enthusiasm. Other aspects of the "working with" process included

- conducting a series of meetings for all participants—children, parents, and members of the community—to describe the project, report on its progress, and solicit input on the accuracy and appropriateness of images and text;
- keeping the tribal governments informed through initial and progress letters;
- seeking and receiving approval from the superintendent of the Northern Pueblo Agency schools;
- forming a panel of elementary school teachers from the pueblos and Santa Fe public schools to provide input on the content, structure, and eventual uses of the book; and
- selecting an advisory group of children, parents, and other community members to participate in final editorial and design decisions.

JACKIE LOPEZ, MICHAEL TAFOYA,
BRUCE HUCKO.
(PHOTO BY BAYLOR CHAPMAN)

PHYSICAL LANDSCAPE

There are nineteen individual pueblos in the Southwest. They include the pueblos of the Rio Grande and Zuni, located in New Mexico, and the Hopi villages in Arizona. They are commonly divided into six distinct language groups: Tiwa, Towa, Tewa, Keresan, Zuni, and Hopi.

The six Tewa-speaking villages are situated in the Rio Grande valley north of Santa Fe and south of Velarde, New Mexico, a distance of about 35 miles. The valley extends from the Sangre de Cristo Mountains in the east to the Jemez Mountains in the west. Prior to the arrival of the Spaniards, all of this region was Tewa. Today it is interrupted by state and county roads, Hispanic land grants, federal lands, and towns with predominantly Hispanic and Anglo populations.

JOSHUA AND JARED NARANJO
AT BLACK MESA

In this high desert country, where the average annual rainfall is fifteen inches, vegetation near the Rio Grande ranges from cottonwood trees and a piñon-juniper forest to cacti and assorted grasses and flowers. At higher elevations there are aspens and evergreens, the latter used in many Pueblo dances to signify life. Mountains are considered sacred, primarily because they are sources of water, the most precious element of life in this dry land. Deer, elk, and bear roam the mountains, while ravens, hawks, and eagles soar across the sky. Below them stretches a loose chain of Tewa communities, each an independent nation with its own government.

San Juan—*Ohkay Ówingeh*, or "Place of the Strong People"—is the northernmost pueblo, sitting where the Chama River empties into the Rio Grande. San Juan has existed in much of its present form since the earliest days of the conquistadors, more than twenty years before the Pilgrims landed at Plymouth Rock.

South of San Juan, on the west side of the Rio Grande, lies the pueblo of Santa Clara. In Tewa it is called *Kha P'oe Ówingeh*, or "Wild Rose Water," in reference to the stream that cascades from the mountains and through the pueblo to the river.

P'owhogeh Ówingeh, "Where the Water Cuts Down Through," aptly describes the pueblo of San Ildefonso. "San I," as the children call it, is situated at the beginning of a deep gorge cut by the Rio Grande into the eastern flank of the Jemez Mountains. Just north of the pueblo is Black Mesa, a volcanic butte where villagers defended themselves from attacks by the Spanish in 1694.

On the western edge of the Sangre de Cristo Mountains is "Mound of Earth in the Corner"—*Nanbe Ówingeh*, or Nambé Pueblo. Inhabited, like most of the other Tewa pueblos, since about AD 1300, Nambé has struggled to maintain its language and ceremonies in the face of a declining population.

The reverence for water that permeates Tewa culture is reflected in the name of Pojoaque Pueblo—*P'osuwägeh Ówingeh*, "Place to Drink Water." Nearly abandoned in 1909, the pueblo today is being energetically reestablished.

Tets'ugeh Ówingeh, or Te Tsu Geh Pueblo, formerly known as Tesuque, is the first of the Tewa pueblos to officially claim use of its proper Tewa name, which means "Cottonwood Tree Place." Warriors from this pueblo were the first to fight in the Pueblo Revolt against Spanish oppression in 1680.

CONDUCTING INTERVIEWS, GATHERING ART

This book was conceived as one in which the children's words would complement their visual art. Over a five-month period, forty children were interviewed individually, with parental permission, for up to ninety minutes each. The conversations recounted here were assembled from taped interviews conducted variously at the child's home, in a tree or clubhouse, sitting outside at sunset, or taking a walk. The children selected for these interviews really chose themselves by displaying naturally confident, thoughtful, playful, and engaging personalities. Each of them, in addition, possesses a well-balanced spirit.

Choosing artwork for this volume from among the several hundred pieces submitted was a very difficult task. Some of the art is from my personal collection. Much of it was produced in school classes, and several pieces were commissioned especially for the book. I made the final "cut" on the bases of quality, diversity of technique, range of age, correlation to text, and the indefinable "WOW!" factor. Image and word use agreements were created and signed by each child. Artists retain copyrights to their imagery.

VALERIE MARTINEZ

"DEAR BRUCE, I CAN'T DRAW YOUR PIG!"

The children call me "art coach." To me, a coach is someone who recognizes and nurtures his players' innate talents so that each can become a vital contributor to the team. In the case of art, the "team" is all of humanity.

You learn a lot about children by watching them paint or draw. You see who is happy and who is not, who is playful or cautious, intuitive or calculating, who has self-confidence and self-esteem. You recognize who has been watching which programs on TV and how video games and movies influence their lives. You see how children view themselves, their families, and their communities. Watching children in a Pueblo school, you start to identify those who feel pride in their people and culture.

Teaching art to children is a dynamic occupation. More than simply offering time, materials, and ideas, it involves nurturing a relationship with individuals. My ideas about coaching art fall into three areas—attitude, skills and concepts, and application.

ATTITUDE

Children's artwork is the heart's work.

I am convinced that children understand that every mark and line they make on paper is connected directly to their hearts and souls. This connection is felt rather than spoken and can be observed in children's behavior, as when Juan concentrates for hours at home on a drawing, when Cami abandons her family to paint in her room, or when Jerome chooses to skip recess so that he may continue painting.

The art-soul connection is also apparent when a child crumples a drawing because it has not met her expectations. It is seen in Genna's frustration when, having tried in vain to draw a favorite animal, she asks me for help and attempts the two or three methods I show her. Then she scribbles a note, slams it on my desk, and returns to her seat, arms folded, brow scrunched. "Dear Bruce, I can't draw your pig!" In this instance, I found a way to make Genna laugh. Then I helped her discover how to make *her* pig.

In order to work successfully with children you must go where they are, learn how to speak their language. And you must be as sensitive to individual emotions as you are knowledgeable about the various media. Being an art coach is an emotionally charged activity. I can't work with children without being moved by them. I place as much importance on developing a relationship of trust and good feeling, fostering what Rollo May calls "the courage to create," as I do on presenting techniques and concepts.

Teaching Pueblo children requires becoming informed about their culture and establishing an environment in which peer help is sought, ideas are respected, and we all try to work together. It is about nurturing the whole child and helping her reach her

ANGELA PACHECO

8

maximum potential. The art in this book is not "Indian art"; rather, it is art produced by children whose Pueblo identity is a part of their total life experience. And it is the expression of that totality that is encouraged in making art.

Each one of us is shaped by the natural, social, political, cultural, temporal, and visual environments in which we grow up. The creation of art with children likewise calls for a special environment if growth is to be successful.

In my role of art coach I strive to create this atmosphere by

- guiding a process of skill development and self-discovery that liberates each child's natural talents;
- viewing the children not as empty vessels to be filled but as young peers bursting with images and experiences;
- understanding that my students have been molded by a landscape and a culture that have endowed them with a unique world view;
- respecting individual points of origin and recognizing that the "Pueblo" or cultural experience is different for each person;
- providing the space, the courage, and a process that will help the children explore themselves and their world;
- instructing them in the body of knowledge called art and how to apply it, always emphasizing process over product; and
- building an environment in which children are not afraid to take risks.

How can we help children reach their potential, not only in art, but as human beings? The real question becomes not whether Genna could draw *my* pig, but rather what prevented her from drawing her own pig.

Time and time again I have heard these refrains from children: "I don't know what to draw. What do I draw? Is this what you want, teacher?" This litany is repeated regularly in classrooms across the United States. To my ear it indicates the presence of a force that stifles a child's innate ability to draw and to achieve personal satisfaction.

TV and video games, commercially successful art, American pop cultural icons. Are these the enemies, or are they simply misunderstood and misused allies? A teacher cannot judge his students' interests and values without the risk of losing their attention. To help children learn, one must start where they are and bring them forward with specific, thoughtful, gentle nudges. In our art classes we connect to language, science, math, and other curriculum areas. We connect to culture and community. Perhaps most of all, we connect to ourselves. My goal in teaching art is not to create a new generation of artists but to help foster a generation of aware, respectful, creative, and positive young people.

SKILLS AND CONCEPTS

Making art is about communicating internally and externally. Art is a language, and Pueblo people speak it well. The elements of design, color, movement, rhythm, balance, and detail are present in many facets of Pueblo life.

We spend a lot of class time learning how to make our materials talk. What can a pencil say? How do I make my paints describe something? Finding out how to control the materials through skills, techniques, and ideas is the essence of my approach. Our drawing work is done primarily with pencils, crayons, colored pencils, charcoal, and oil pastels as we explore shading, shadowing, sketching, and texture. We draw our hands, our bedrooms, and grandma's pottery. We learn to make eye contact with the subject, observe the wealth of subjects around us, and trust our eyes to get form right.

In painting and printing we use watercolors, liquid tempera, and inks to learn about value, blending colors, and the expressive power of brush strokes. We may try to match the color of adobe on one day and paint "a horse of a different color" the next. With elementary school children, the goal is not to have them master skills so much as to open their minds to the available options and encourage them to make their own choices.

We begin the school year with seeing and drawing and progress to painting and printmaking. The images we make span the continuum from the literal to the abstract. Personal creativity is enhanced through exercises in imagination. A realistic drawing of a hammer, for instance, becomes a "tool pet" through the addition of arms and legs, texture, and background. A mountain of dirty clothes takes the place of trees on a mountainside by simply changing textures. Extraordinary things happen as we first learn the rules and then learn to bend them.

A good teacher is also part confidante, magician, entertainer, counselor, and psychiatrist. An example: A roomful of second- and third-graders are trying to find the right combination of colors to illustrate *My Grandfather's Blue Horse*, a humorous story by San Juan elder Esther Martinez that illustrates the many applications of the Tewa word for blue. The children in this tale are asked by their grandfather to bring home a "dirty blue horse," but they can't seem to find a horse that is the right color.

I designed this project as a lesson in creating depth and mixing colored pencils. Each child first chose a part of the story to illustrate. We learned, from looking at favorite picture books, how to make the main subject large on the paper while keeping less important elements small. We've added detail, and our drawings are now ready for color.

On this day I had asked some of the kids to come to class dressed all in blue. We have collected all the blue crayons, pastels, pencils, and paints we can find. We study the differences between colors. None of them fits the class's notion of "dirty blue."

"HORSE IN THE WIND"
IAN CARLISLE, AGE 11
OIL PASTEL

I've set them up. In a moment of inspiration the day before, I bought a bag of blue corn chips, two of which are now tucked away in the pocket of my blue workshirt. I begin the class by talking about being at home the night before, looking for blue things. As I talk, I begin to eat one of the blue corn chips. No one says a thing. I turn my attention to the art room and mention each of the blue objects it contains. "But naaah, that's not quite the right color," I say each time. And then, bringing the second chip to my mouth, I exclaim, "Hey! Look at this!" as though I'd never seen it before. "Check out its color! What would you call that?"

"Blue!" calls a child.

"Dirty blue!" shouts another.

"Just like our horse!" exclaims someone else.

"You shouldn't eat in front of kids!" scolds one of the girls. In the verbal melee that ensues, I pull out the hidden bag of chips and dump small handfuls on each worktable. "Use all your colors. Try to match the chips," I direct amid the pandemonium of "I only got two!" One of the children finds a combination that works: indigo blue, deep red, and brown. All of them grab for colors and finish their horses. The results are stunning. "That was fun!" exclaims Angela Pacheco, crunching the last chip. Work and play have merged to create learning.

APPLICATION

A child's mind holds a wealth of wonderful images. Technical skills can help release them, but even more important are time and encouragement for children to apply their newly acquired skills to an image of their own creation.

The four sample lessons included in this book demonstrate some of the ways in which an assignment originates and develops. I hope these brief descriptions and hands-on instructions will serve as prototypes to inspire teachers, parents, and kids to devise other fun art projects.

After an exercise or two in a particular skill I generally guide the children in making "a real piece of art." For instance, from studying the creation of values using tempera paint, they learn that adding white lightens a given color while adding black darkens it. After exhibiting their control of this technique in an exercise, it is time to begin work on a project that requires several class sessions. Sometimes I let the children paint anything they want as long as they show me they are using the new skill. More often I guide the image development with questions: "Where do you see value used in the real world? What kinds of pictures could we make using value?" Through this dialogue, we define our project.

JOE SUAZO

"The sky is different values of blue!" Project: Paint the sky in a range of values using one or more colors. In the distance, add a mountain of all dark values and a foreground of rocks, grass, water, or something else using only medium and light values.

"When you see sun on one side of the house and shadow on the other, is that value?" Project: Draw your house from an angle so you can see several sides. Show how sunshine hits it, using light paint values for sun and dark for shadow.

I try to keep individual minds active by constantly roaming the room, asking questions, and making comments: "What can you do in this corner? Hey! That's a wonderful color. How did you make it? If you outline that in a dark color it might show up better. What is it you're trying to say here so I can help you figure out how to do it? This is neat! Can I show the class?"

Don't talk too much. Just do your show!" pleads fourth-grader Danielle Martinez as I carry supplies into the classroom and prepare to introduce a lesson. Danielle knows I like to talk out the idea first, get the kids verbally and mentally charged, before they settle down to work. Clearly, she would prefer to get her materials and be turned loose. Well, in this book, the time has come for Danielle and the others to do *their* show!

Making art is hard work. Pueblo children have provided the heart, energy, and inspiration for this book. In return, the book honors the Tewa children and communities who practice the greatest art of all: the art of living.

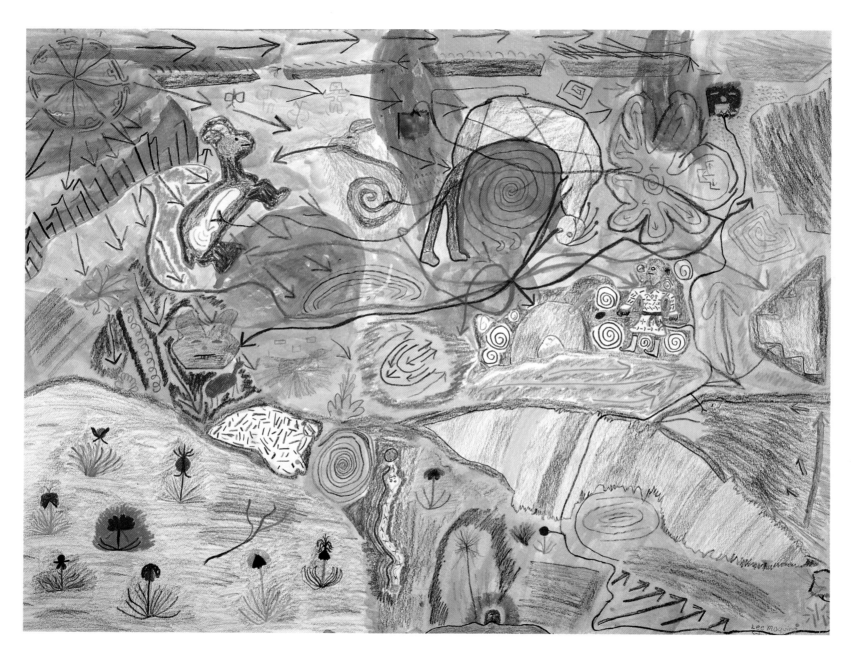

"ANCIENT ANCESTORS"
LEE MOQUINO, AGE 10
COLORED PENCIL, WATERCOLOR

They Set the Pace for Us

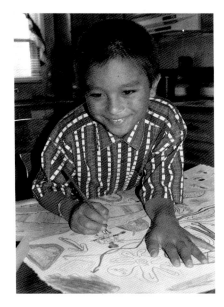

LEE MOQUINO

L EE MOQUINO HUNCHES over a large sheet of watercolor paper on the porch of his great-grandmother's house. A light spring breeze stirs the new leaves of the cottonwood trees, and colorful flowers bloom in the garden. Lee's "granny" lives on a quiet dirt road near the pueblo of San Ildefonso. He visits her often, for they are best friends.

A thoughtful and sensitive young man, eight-year-old Lee makes marks on paper with oil pastel and pencil similar to those that have been made in this landscape for more than a thousand years. "I like to make different kinds of drawings about our native cultures," he says quietly. "Sometimes I'll draw pottery, but if it doesn't come out good I get mad and throw it away.

"I also like to draw petroglyphs. They make me go back, way back in time . . ." Lee's voice trails off as he gazes into the sky. "It makes me daydream about how it would be if I was alive then. It would be neat. You'd have to fight a lot, though, which would be kind of boring. I like to draw the kokopelli, the flute player. I like how he plays the flute and how he can carry all kinds of things at once."

Lee pauses and deftly changes colors, working alternately in pastel and pencil. "To do good art you've got to think about your own culture, what you're into, what you like the most. My brain comes up with Indian things like feathers, dancing things, and petroglyphs. That's what I'm into—social studies."

NAOMI NARANJO

ANCESTRAL HISTORY

To understand Tewa children and their art, we too must go "way back in time." The children's art is grounded in the Pueblo people's past. For many centuries the American Southwest was inhabited by a people commonly called the Anasazi. These ancestral Pueblo people are known to the Tewa as *sedaa*—"our ancient ancestors." They left a rich legacy of artifacts, home sites, and rock art in what is now the Four Corners area, where New Mexico, Arizona, Utah, and Colorado meet.

Archaeologists tell us that in approximately AD 1250 these people built the great houses at Mesa Verde, Chaco Canyon, and Canyon de Chelly. A hundred years later they built homes near the Rio Grande north of Santa Fe, New Mexico, at the sites that are now Bandelier National Monument and Puyé Cliffs, a Santa Clara Pueblo tribal park. In the mountains, canyons, and mesas of this region are a dozen or more other villages built and abandoned by the ancestral Pueblo people.

Tewa cultural history tells a different story. Long ago the Tewa lived in a world beneath Sandy Place Lake. It was a dark world inhabited by supernatural beings as well as humans and animals. Death was unknown there. The "first mothers" of all the Tewa, Blue Corn Woman (Summer) and White Corn Maiden (Winter), asked one of the men to search for a way for the people to leave the lake. On his fourth try, the man found the way. After several attempts, the people entered this world and created a great village that is said to be near present-day Ojo Caliente. Eventually the people left in groups to establish the six modern Tewa pueblos we know today. Since San Juan was founded first, it is sometimes referred to as the "mother pueblo" and is headquarters for the Eight Northern Indian Pueblos Council.

Pueblo history is embedded in the land, and thoughts of the ancestors persist in the minds of the young. "I think our ancestors are really important in our lives because they set the tradition. They set the pace for us," says twelve-year-old Naomi Naranjo. In Naomi's home in San Ildefonso, basketball and school achievement awards share wall space with her paintings. Like many children who have been taught their cultural past, Naomi has particular opinions about her ancestors.

"They were really strict, which was good. Nowadays kids can go anywhere, but back then they had to stay home, do their chores, and learn their language. Now we have to carry that on. We stumble a little because sometimes we don't listen to the elder ones."

The people of San Ildefonso trace their immediate ancestry to the people who lived in the cliff dwellings of Frijoles Canyon (now Bandelier National Monument). The opportunity to see and sense that ancestry so closely offers children from "San I" a unique perspective on their history.

"Sometimes I go with my mom when she demonstrates pottery making at Bandelier," says Naomi. "I walk around and look at all the caves. One time we went to Mesa Verde because that's where the Old People were, too. The rangers let us into a kiva that hadn't had many people in it. It was real special to us because nothing was moved and we could see everything."

"I've been to Bandelier millions of times," claims Devonna Naranjo, "just to look around and have picnics." Known to her relatives as "Dee," this energetic eight-year-old slows down when she talks about the past. "They had to hunt for their stuff and it wasn't as easy as it is for us. They had to work for what they wanted and what they needed. It would have been hard to live then."

Cousins Heather, age thirteen, Tricia, and Justin Dasheno, both ten, can usually be found at their grandparents' house in Santa Clara, watching TV or helping with the chores. Time seems to collapse when they speak of their ancestors, as if the children were actually living then.

"I wonder how they caught their food, if they had to run for it, and how it would be if it was cold," says Justin.

"They used to have long dances," adds Tricia. "They drew pictures. They had a better kiva and taller houses made out of clay."

LYDIA MARTINEZ AND
MICHAEL TAFOYA AT
SAN JUAN PETROGLYPHS

"They were probably nice, never mean to each other, and everyone got along," says Heather. "They were kind enough to leave us a lot of good habits. Our grandparents and parents are trying to teach us those things so we can survive."

Santa Clara Pueblo maintains the Puyé Cliff Dwellings in Santa Clara Canyon. Most Santa Clara children visit the site for family picnics or with parents who demonstrate arts and crafts for tourists.

"I like going to Puyé because I find nickels there. And I like to see if I can fit in some of the smaller dwellings," says twelve-year-old KhaPovi Harvier. "I wonder who could have been small enough to fit in them. I see where people have carved things like 'John and Laura,' and I wonder if that's where they made out."

"I think about how many differences there were a long time ago and how life has changed a lot," adds Jordan Harvier, KhaPovi's thirteen-year-old brother. "I think about the way we used to dress, the way we used to gather food and make weapons. I'm curious about how the people survived. I respect them for passing the culture on to their children and then on to the present."

This sense of continuity, of carrying on the work, customs, and meanings of the ancestors, is important to Pueblo people. Preserving traditional knowledge is a most crucial element in the process of sustaining cultural and personal vitality.

Along the western bank of the Rio Grande, north of San Juan Pueblo, are hundreds of drawings made on rocks and cliffs by ancestral Pueblo people. San Juan children delight in climbing among the boulders to find examples of rock art and speculate about their creators.

"I think that they really, really loved art, 'cause you find all kinds of Indian designs," says Jackie Lopez. With her love of reading, she sees connections that others may overlook. "In Chinese writing there are all kinds of signs for talking. Maybe this is the same. Maybe they are saying, 'Here is my pueblo. These are the animals that we respect.'"

Daniel Archuleta listens patiently, nods in agreement, and adds, "They draw to tell you about who they are and maybe what their name is. They tell what kind of animals lived around here and what animals they hunted. They prayed to the animals, thanking them for giving meat and hides so the people could eat and make something to wear, just like we do now."

"When I look at the drawings I wonder who drew them. Was it a lady, a man, or an animal?" muses ten-year-old Lydia Martinez. "Maybe there was nobody to talk to so they made pictures for somebody else to discover and try and figure out where they went." The scattered remnants of culture remain a puzzle for all of us.

"I think they were kind of confused, because it was a new land. They were trying to decide 'Where should we stay?' or 'Should we move on?'" suggests Naomi. "They liked to travel, but once they found a place to stay they stayed there and started the tradition. That's what I think."

"YOUNG KOKOPELLI"
JOE SUAZO, AGE 7
WATERCOLOR

"HORNED SUN DESIGN"
AMANDA NARANJO, AGE 11
COLORED PENCIL, WATERCOLOR

"They were very strong and powerful, and they could do anything they wanted. Like they could make it rain or they could put a curse on you, make your house fall down," states Katie Weahkee. She sees something else in the rock art: "It's like they are coming after us real soon, like they are going to pick all of us up and take us to another world."

GRANDPARENTS AS A LINK TO THE PAST

For many Pueblo children the past is not so very far away—a walk next door, a bike ride through the quiet streets of the village. Pueblo children are blessed with grandparents and even great-grandparents who live in the same community. Many children are raised, completely or in part, by their grandparents. In their grandparents' homes they learn about the past through stories and practices others have long forgotten. Grandparents also teach their grandchildren to use the Tewa language.

Nowadays, their role is mixed. Once the keepers of story and tradition, today's grandparents can also be found engaged in modern activities. From bingo to bowling, fishing to farming, grandparents still set a pace that is a challenge for the young to follow.

"Well, they won't tell you anything unless you ask them," says Naomi, with a note of respect and love in her voice. "Like my grandma from here, she's more into today than 'used to be.' But if you just ask her she'll tell you what happened. My grandpa's more into '70s music. He also likes those old songs, like 'Oh, Susanna,' that one, with a banjo on my knee? If you go in his truck that's all you listen to. But when you're in his pottery room, that's where he thinks about most of this Pueblo stuff, that's where he paints, and he'll tell you all about why you paint this or what something represents."

"My grandma taught me how to sew," says Devonna with pride, "and she taught me how to get her a Coke. She'd give me fifty cents and I'd go get a Coke for her. My grandpa was good at telling stories and getting on my grandma's nerves! He liked to sing songs, Baptist church songs. The stories were about how he used to go up to the canyon and hunt. Grandma Rose sings Indian songs and tells stories, too."

Like many Tewa children, Devonna lives just minutes away from an extended family of grandmother, aunts, and uncles. Devonna's mother, Theresa, appreciates her family's help in raising her daughter.

"We were pretty young when she was born, so she got to spend time with aunts and other relatives, especially grandparents. All of her dad's brothers and sisters are artists, and her great-grandmother is a potter. Devonna would see her working on pottery almost every day when she was little. I think she felt very happy going back and forth getting to know people. I think what's really key for a little kid is to have someone who is really interested in you, who listens to you, talks patiently with you, and invests time in you."

KATIE WEAHKEE

THE STORY OF THE DEER BOY

From the legacy of the ancestral Pueblo people a vibrant culture has emerged, one that provides its children with a deep connection to the earth. Traditional stories bring the past into the present as storytellers like Esther Martinez of San Juan Pueblo carry the oral tradition forward. This is one story that she tells.

Once, it is said, the deer living on the east mesa were unhappy because they had eaten almost all of their grass. They could see lots of fresh grass growing on the west mesa across the river and decided to go there. To do so they had to pass through the village. Led by a big buck they passed quietly through the village at dawn and neared the river. There they heard a strange sound. They walked closer and found a baby boy wrapped in a blanket. He was crying. The leader of the deer gathered the baby boy up in his antlers and told the others that they must take care of him and teach him the way of the deer. They crossed the river and went on with their lives.

Several years later some of the village men went to the mountains to collect firewood. They heard something approaching and hid behind trees and bushes. It was the Deer Boy. Even though he walked on two feet like a human boy, in every other way he was a deer. He ate like a deer. He moved like a deer. He thought like a deer. The men returned to the pueblo, told their elders what they had seen, and asked them what to do. They were instructed to capture the Deer Boy and bring him to the kiva.

The men returned to the mountains and set a trap for the Deer Boy. He came again and the men caught him. They tied him up with strong ropes and took him into the kiva. The elders said that they must keep the Deer Boy in the kiva for four days. After that time he would return to being a human boy.

Everything went well for the first three nights. The fire was warm, the boy was fed, and the guard stayed awake. But on the last night, the guard fell asleep. He heard a sound and woke up to see the boy climbing the ladder that led out of the kiva. As soon as he stepped outside the Deer Boy turned into a real deer and ran into the mountains. The men called for him to return, but he did not.

DANIEL ARCHULETA, CENTER,
DEER DANCE, SAN JUAN PUEBLO

Every February at San Juan Pueblo, more than one hundred men and boys dance the Deer Dance. They come down from the hills before dawn and cross the highway. Clad in moccasins, white leggings, embroidered dance kilts, bells, jewelry, and armbands that hold evergreen boughs, and wearing headdresses of painted yucca topped with real deer antlers, they walk toward the village. They walk like deer. They *are* deer.

The dance recalls the story of the Deer Boy and honors the Pueblo people's connection to the deer. The dance thanks the deer for giving their lives so that the people can have food and clothing.

21

"DEER DANCER"
FRANKIE TAPIA, AGE 7
WATERCOLOR

Dancing continues throughout the day Late in the afternoon, just before the last dance, the deer exchange the straight, feather-topped poles they've been holding for two short sticks. Leaning forward on these sticks, the dancers truly look like four-legged deer. The drum beats very, very slowly. There is no singing. The deer dance very, very slowly. Women and girls from the pueblo move closer to the deer, surrounding them. The men who guard the dancers tell them to step back. There is excitement. There is anticipation. Suddenly there is a gunshot. The deer flee.

"I was six years old when I first danced the Deer," says Daniel Archuleta, smiling as he remembers. "I felt nervous because my grandma told me to run at the end of the dance. When they shot the gun all the ladies were ganging up and trying to catch me. This one lady tried to catch me but I just went under her legs because I was so tiny. Then I fell and she caught me and took me to her house and I ate and the day was nice. This year I got away, but when I came back up from the river these ladies caught me. It's harder now 'cause I can't go under anyone's legs!"

It is the job of the women and girls to capture the deer, take them home, and feed them. The deer then return to their own homes as men and boys. It is said that those men and boys who are not caught cannot return to the village but must spend the rest of their lives as deer in the mountains. The children tell stories of this happening. The children know that such things are true.

Stories bind the generations together. Jackie Lopez of San Juan has listened well. "Something I learned from my grandparents is to respect all men, women, and living things," she says. "My grandparents also tell me stories about the old days. Once a snake lived in the kiva, a great big bull snake. One day he got loose and they thought he would go

"THE BREADMAKER"
POVI TAFOYA, AGE 11
TEMPERA, WATERCOLOR

around eating all the children. They trapped him in the kiva and then they used fire to burn him and blow him up. The snake's skin covered the rocks and made that black color. They built the chapel there, and that's why part of the chapel is black."

KhaPovi and Jordan Harvier sit atop their pottery shed in Santa Clara Pueblo. It's fall and the sun is setting on the mountains, turning them deep pink. The children's easy going, subtle humor and honesty invite friendship. Both are strong, independent personalities who enjoy the company of several grandparents.

"They tell me about the past and how different it was when they were young. They would listen to the radio or tell stories and make things to entertain themselves," says Jordan. "My grandpa likes to work a lot. He's always trying to make his yard look good."

"These days a lot of elders go to bingo," KhaPovi adds. "I think it's just a waste of time and money, especially if they don't win. And of course, I don't follow my own advice and I go, too!"

As a result of the growing influence of non-Indian culture in the pueblos, traditional values have become vulnerable to neglect and abandonment. Some children regard participation in ceremonial dances or other involvement in Pueblo life as "boring." Others are able to maintain a dynamic balance between the two worlds. With many parents adopting "modern" jobs and lifestyles in order to provide for their families, grandparents become an important cultural link between the past, the present, and the future.

Daniel Archuleta lives with his grandma at San Juan Pueblo. "She taught me responsibility," he says. "She taught me to be generous and respect others, to say hello and shake their hands and tell them my name. There's a couple of older people at the pueblo who taught me how to make rattles and drums, and others who taught me how to do carvings."

"Grandparents tell us what's right and wrong, and how to speak our language. They do things for us. They are always there when you need them," says Heather.

"They told us, 'When you have your children, you will tell them what we tell to you,'" adds Tricia. "They taught us our stories, our language. My grandma taught me how to cook. It was popcorn in a pan! My grandpa taught me how to cut wood and make pots, and my uncle taught me about our culture."

Famous artists, tribal leaders, holders of traditional knowledge, singers, and drummers—all the titles that can be bestowed on the elders fall aside at day's end. Then they are just people.

"I like my grandparents when it's time to go to bed," says Jackie Lopez wistfully. "They hug me and tuck me in. They are all nice at the end."

"GRANDMOTHER'S CORN"
DEVONNA NARANJO, AGE 9
TEMPERA

Many of the children in Devonna's third-grade class have grandparents and great-grandparents who live nearby. I wanted to strengthen the connection between them while we worked on a new skill: painting with kitchen sponges instead of brushes.

"Today we're going to paint without a brush!" I say as I enter the classroom.

"How are we going to do that?" the children wonder.

"How about a sponge?" I say, holding up an ordinary kitchen sponge. We brainstorm about how to use it: dipping it into one or more colors at a time, cutting it into shapes, using the flat surface and the thin edge for different thicknesses.

"What are we going to paint?"

"Your grandparents," I say.

"Aaaaah. I don't want to," the class responds with a moan.

"Well, not their faces, but some object that reminds you of them. When you think of your grandmother or grandfather, what do you see them with? What are they usually doing or using that you could paint?" The class begins to stir with interest.

"Choose one object that you can paint large and simple. Experiment with your sponge to make different textures."

I approach Devonna, who is working in her customary pensive manner. A curious image appears on her paper.

"Does your grandmother use corn a lot?" I ask.

"My grandmother *is* corn!" she replies emphatically.

Corn is revered as a life-giving substance among the Pueblo people, so powerful that it is often referred to as "Grandmother." No doubt Devonna's grandmother, Rose, plays an equally vital role in her life. In one image Devonna was able to express an important relationship between herself, her culture, and her grandmother.

DO IT!

What object comes to mind when you think of your grandparents? It may be something they wear, a tool they use often, an activity they are always engaged in, or something they own that you know is important to them. Draw the object so it fills the paper and color it in with whatever materials you have. Add details and create a simple color or design background. When you are finished, share your image with your family and grandparents.

25

"RAIN POND"
DANIELLE MARTINEZ, AGE 9
WATERCOLOR

My Name Is a Secret

DANIELLE MARTINEZ

Blue Summer. *Paayo Tsáwá.*
White Blowing Snow. *Pho Phedeh Ts'aa.*
Red Mountain. *K'uu Pi P'in.*
Sun Mountain Shaking. *Than P'in Ayan.*
Star Flower. *Agóyó Póvi.*
Cloud Flower. *Oku Póvi.*
Shining Lake. *P'oekwi Tsawá.*
Turtle. *Oekuu.*

ANOTHER LINK BETWEEN the children and their culture is their Tewa names. When a child is born it is given an English, or "proper," name. After that, parents and other relatives may bestow one or more Tewa names. These names connect the children to their ancestry and the landscape of home in a powerful way.

"In the old days they used to give kids the older peoples' names," says Naomi Naranjo. "Nowadays they'll say, 'Oh, we'll just think of a name.' It doesn't come from anywhere; maybe it just sounds nice. But sometimes, if they want the kid to grow up in a certain way, and the grandparents are real serious about the name, they'll have someone important pick it. They'll say, 'This is why we give it to you. We want you to grow up strong.'

"My grandma gave me my name, *Oku Póvi.* It means Cloud Flower. It says something about me because the clouds are way up in the sky, and here I am real tall, taller than my older sister and my mom. Or it might mean I have to conquer something, 'cause the sky is way up there and I have to try to reach it."

Tewa names can come from various sources—the name of a sacred mountain, a natural event, an early behavior of the child, or a respected ancestor. Often the name is connected to the particular clan—Summer or Winter—that a child is associated with.

"My name is *Pho P'oekwin*," says Angela Pacheco. "It means Snow Coming Down and a Lake."

"Mine is *Oyégi P'oekwin*," says her younger sister, Christine. "It means Ice River with Frost Coming Down."

"My Indian name is *Agóyó Póvi*," says Jackie Lopez. "It means Star Flower. I got it when I was six. My grandma took us next door where a lady named Theresa was naming the kids. We all had to bring something to feed our tribal members. I was wearing a white blouse, 'cause you're supposed to, and I was carrying hot cocoa, and it spilled all over my blouse. My grandma was mad! My mom, too. She made me go change and said, 'This time don't drop it!' They had so many kids to give names to that we left and called Theresa up instead. So I got my Indian name over the phone."

JACKIE LOPEZ

Jackie is an exuberant child, full of vigor and ready to talk about almost anything. We visit in the living room of her parents' tidy double-wide trailer. She is all smiles as she finishes telling me about her name.

"I'm a Summer child. My grandmother's name is *Póvi* [flower], my mom's name is *Than Póvi*, and mine is *Agóyó Póvi*, so we all have flowers in our names. And as for the star part, I'm a star that shines up in the sky!"

At a traditional Tewa birth there are usually two midwives in attendance: the "naming mother" and her assistant. These women take over the mother's care from the time labor starts until four days after the birth. During this period both mother and child remain indoors and receive visits from relatives and friends. Each visitor symbolically gathers in, with both hands, all illness and misfortune that may befall the child and casts them to the west, "beyond Mount Tsikomo, to the land of the Navajo"— the traditional enemies of the Tewa people.

At dawn on the fourth day after birth, the midwives take the newborn child outside to present her to the sun and bestow a name on her. Just as the sun's first rays appear over the Sangre de Cristo Mountains, the naming mother holds the infant and two perfect ears of corn—one white, one blue—representing Blue Corn Woman and White Corn Maiden. Meanwhile her assistant makes a sweeping inward

"DAUGHTER OF THE SUN"
HEATHER DASHENO, AGE 11
COLORED PENCIL

motion over them with a hand broom to gather in blessings for the child. Infant and corn are presented in turn to each of the six directions—east, south, west, north, sky, and earth—while a prayer is said.

Then the naming mother bestows the name, invoking Blue Corn Woman and White Corn Maiden. They are the original mothers who were with the people before their emergence into this world. It is from them that children acquire their souls at birth. The name a child receives during this ceremony is the one by which she will be known to the village for the rest of her life.

VICTORIA MARTINEZ

I enter San Ildefonso Pueblo on a clear day in June and drive along quiet dirt roads past the dance plazas and stands of shady cottonwoods. Thin smoke trails from a yard; someone must be firing pottery. Soon I arrive at the home of twelve-year-old Victoria Martinez, who greets me at the door and invites me in. We sit at the dining-room table with her parents, Linda and Dale. Linda has set out some treats: Pueblo fruit cookies and tea.

When I ask Victoria about her Indian name, she says she doesn't know it. Her parents look surprised. I pose the question again: "What's your Tewa name?" and now a smile of understanding appears on Victoria's face. I had confused her by using the word "Indian" instead of "Tewa."

She tells me, "My Tewa name is *Póvi Baá*—Flower Belt. I got it from my godparents when I was baptized. When was that?" she asks her parents.

"Two days after you came home from the hospital," Linda replies. "They came before the sun rose. Grandmother Adelphia had a beautiful woven belt with flowers in it that had been given to her, and Victoria got that for her name."

Some weeks later Adelphia herself tells me that *Póvi Baá* is also the name of one of the hills from which the Deer dancers emerge on the morning of San Ildefonso's Feast Day. This image evokes Victoria. The deer arrive like dawn, quiet and strong. Their presence, like hers, brings a good feeling.

Every Tewa name has a story attached to it. The story provides the named child with some personal history and insight into his own character.

"I'M A FLYING FRED"
FRED MARTINEZ, AGE 8
TEMPERA

31

"THE HEART OF OHKAY ÓWINGEH"
DANIEL ARCHULETA, AGE 12
COLORED PENCIL

Daniel Archuleta's Tewa name holds special significance for him. "*O'kuu Taa* means Striped Turtle," he explains. "It came from my dad, who was born right when they started dancing the Turtle Dance. They wanted me to carry on his name. I think my name is about power. It's like something hit me and striped my shell. Or taking the whips. I have the power to take whatever hits me."

"*P'ink'úwá* is a nickname given to me by my great-grandfather," says eight-year old Jerome Tafoya. "It means Mountain Goat. My *ta* called me that because when I was small I would jump from chair to chair." Jerome's name still holds meaning, for this bright and inquisitive youngster jumps from one creative thought to another, from one prank to another, just as he once jumped from chair to chair.

"Little Feather. That's me!" exclaims Katie Weahkee. "My grandpa gave me that name. When I was little he thought of me as a feather, 'cause I was light and I was neat and I was pretty!"

A number of the children have water- or rain-related names. These signify that the spirits are especially pleased with the child. In this desert environment, water in any form is a blessing.

"My name is *Kua P'oekwin*, Rain Pond, 'cause I look like a raindrop!" says Danielle Martinez, laughing. "I think, too, that when I was born it was raining and the ponds were flooding and when I came home it was raining."

"My name's kind of like that!" says Pam Cata, with a similar smile spreading across her face. "It's *P'oekwi' Tsáwá,*. Shining Lake. My godmother gave me that name because I used to like playing in water and sitting in mud puddles."

"My grandpa named me after my dad," says Lee Moquino quietly. "His name is Cloud. I'm Rain Cloud. *Po Qua a Qua*. When I was little, and even now, I cry a lot," he adds with a thoughtful shrug.

DANIEL ARCHULETA

33

"I'm *Oegée*, which means Ice," says Mauricia Chavarria with her characteristic good humor, "because when my mom brought me home from the hospital it was snowing and there was ice. So my uncle named me Ice."

KhaPovi says, "I have three Tewa names: Blue Duck, Star Stick Flower, and the one I am known by, *KháPóvi*. It means Wild Rose. I am wild with the green, I have to spend whatever money I have! My double-great-aunt gave me my names. I asked my grandma Harvier why I have my name, and she said maybe it's because I am pretty like a rose!"

KhaPovi's brother, Jordan, was also given three names—Turquoise Mountain, Snowbird, and Cloud Designs. Jordan explains, "My great-great-aunt was thinking of all the possible names and probably saw the mountain early in the morning. Snowbird fits me because my dad tells me I was born in a blizzard. My name Cloud Design also fits because I like to draw all kinds of designs."

Nathana Bird flies through the air and lands with a thump in the sandy arroyo behind her house at San Juan Pueblo. Nathana is a bundle of focused energy whose smile radiates all the warmth of the sun. What would her Tewa name be?

"*Oekúua Sáwin*—Cloud with a Mark on It," she says joyously. "My grandpa and grandma gave it to me. It's very, very favorite to me 'cause it was my grandma's name."

Nathana's older brother, Barney, says simply, "My name is . . . a secret."

Land and people. People and land. The relationship between the two is eternally binding. Home is where they meet, and home and family are reflected in one's name.

NATHANA BIRD

34

My name sits
on the soft, smooth lake.
My voice sounds like
gentle rain
falling from the sky, hitting me
like hard, strong lightning.
When the cold wind comes
I will flow
from place to place.
My name is soft,
soft like a big, flat quilt.

A few winter days pass,
singing birds are looking
for juicy worms,
blooming flowers grow.
Life comes back,
back into me.
Flowers grow and trees
fall on me.

I am *P'oekwin Póvi*.
I am Lake Flower.
If you look into me
you will see
a beautiful person.
You will see
yourself.

—*Toni Herrera*

"LAKE FLOWER"
TONI HERRERA, AGE 10
OIL PASTEL, TEMPERA

35

ART LESSON: PAINTING YOUR PERSONALITY

"But I might look dumb!" is the dismayed reaction of the class when I introduce the idea of painting self-portraits. I show them a variety of portraits, beginning with photographs and realistic paintings.

"I can't do that!" they exclaim.

I keep pulling out more images, gradually moving from the literal to the abstract: Modigliani, Van Gogh, John Nieto, Helen Hardin, Picasso.

"That's weird!" someone says.

"I get it," says another. "It doesn't have to look just like us, only a little."

"Right!" I reply, explaining that this is a personality portrait. "So you want to use your inside colors, those that you feel say something about you."

After a lesson in drawing facial features, the children get right to work. Most of them tend toward realism. I delight in watching Sophia Lovato apply layer after layer of paint to her portrait. She works with effortless and comfortable abandon.

"There I am!" she proclaims proudly as she finishes.

"SELF-PORTRAIT"
SOPHIA LOVATO, AGE 8
TEMPERA

DO IT!

Make a face shape that almost fills the paper. Put in your eyes, nose, mouth, ears, and neck. Do not add hair yet. Now add the details: eyelids, eyelashes, tear ducts, eyebrows, pupils, and so on. For the nose add nostrils. Add your upper and lower lips and your teeth if you show your mouth open. Remember, you can choose where to place each of these facial elements. Where do yours belong according to your personality?

Remember that your self-portrait does not have to look like you, but it should *feel* like you. You are trying to express your personality on paper, rather than duplicate your skin and bones.

You don't have to color yourself as you really are, either. Paint your inside colors, the colors that you feel like. Put patterns and designs on your face. Finally, add hair. What color will yours be? What does this portrait say about your personality?

"THE AMY PICTURE"
AMY WILLOW, AGE 5
WATERCOLOR

"MY BROTHER AND I"
JASON SERRANO, AGE 6
WATERCOLOR

37

"LOOKING EAST"
KIMBERLY SISNEROS, AGE 11
WATERCOLOR, COLORED PENCIL

A Pueblo Is Where Your Family Is

PAIGE AND NATANNI MIRABAL

"**A** PUEBLO, A PUEBLO, A PUEBLO," sings five-year-old Paige Mirabal, laughing loudly. Something in the word makes Paige sing. But what is a pueblo? When I ask, I am questioned in return: "What do you mean? The people, the village, or the whole thing?"—for the word has multiple meanings.

WHAT IS A PUEBLO?

"It came from the Spanish word meaning 'little village,'" says twelve-year-old Audrey Lujan.

"And little town," adds her best friend, Julie Vigil.

"Little town on the prairie," Audrey says.

"Little pueblo on the prairie," Julie shoots back, and everybody laughs.

The three of us are leaning against the shaded back of a boarded-up building next to Santa Clara Day School. Soon the girls will graduate and leave the pueblo to attend middle school. So, what does the pueblo mean to you? I ask.

"Indians. Traditional dances. Traditional clothes. Traditional feasts," says Julie with a roll of her eyes, exaggerating the word "traditional." "Traditional parties. Traditional tourists."

"A pueblo is a village where all Native American people come from," states Larissa Aguilar from San Ildefonso.

Devonna Naranjo says, "It's a place for visitors to look and get a 'hang' of this community."

"It's a place where you do work," says Natanni Mirabal quietly. Natanni lives with his sisters, Paige and Nakiva, and their parents at Nambé Pueblo. Half of their land and buildings are devoted to their father's stone sculpture studio. Dozens of large pieces of alabaster and granite are scattered across the grounds, waiting to be worked. The children's own sculptures can be found on shelves and tables in the exhibit and work areas. The Mirabal children understand the word "work"; it is something that goes on around them constantly, and they naturally participate in it.

Sisters Danielle Martinez and Mauricia Chavarria live at Santa Clara Pueblo with their grandparents, both of whom are active as artists and participants in Pueblo ceremonies. The two girls exhibit a strong bond with their culture.

We sit on the carpeted floor of their living room. Apart from the large console TV against one wall, just about everything in the room, from the pictures on the walls to the rugs on the floor, speaks of Indian culture. A cottonwood drum hangs in the corner, and Grandma's pottery collection occupies a cabinet and several other shelves.

DANIELLE MARTINEZ AND
MAURICIA CHAVARRIA

Mauricia and Danielle are two years apart in age and often break into and complete each other's sentences. When I pose my question, Danielle begins.

"A pueblo is where our ancestors lived . . ."

"And where we have feasts and Indian dances . . ."

"And where we show our traditional ways . . ."

"And our traditional Indian dances. Finish the question, Bob," says Mauricia, grinning and thrusting the mini-recorder at her younger sister in a parody of a TV news commentator.

"Bob?" I query.

"I think so," Mauricia giggles.

"THE BARN YARD"
VALERIE MARTINEZ, AGE 8
WATERCOLOR

"GRANDMA'S MAILBOX"
ANGELINA NARANJO, AGE 10
WATERCOLOR

HOW WILL I KNOW I'M THERE?

Like any other neighborhood, a pueblo has its distinguishing landmarks. Jerome Tafoya, age eight, lives with his family in Santa Clara and spends much of his time riding his bike around the pueblo. "If you see some trees, fields, and adobe houses, then that's the pueblo," Jerome explains.

"And you'll see ovens, we call them *pantehs*, and maybe if you get there on a certain day you'll see Indian dances," says Lee Moquino. "You'll see the kivas and . . . a bunch of loose dogs!" he concludes, his eyes sparkling.

"Look for the words on the post office," suggests Nathana Bird.

"Look for a big, old church and a kiva," adds Pam Cata.

Pueblos are customarily associated with adobe architecture, a traditional form of building popular in the southwestern United States. Thick walls rise out of the earth to remind Pueblo people of their connection to the land. Adobe houses have practical aspects as well. They stay warm in winter, cool in summer. And the materials are all around you, just waiting to be assembled.

"Indian houses are made of adobe and vigas, big logs of wood that go across the ceiling," says Jackie Lopez. "Other houses have pointy roofs, but ours are flat."

Katie Weahkee explains how adobe bricks are made: "They put some mud and hay together into little blocks. After a while they put them in an oven and let them dry for about an hour. Then they take them out and stack them together to make the house. They plaster the top together and after that they put in the windows and doors."

The architecture of today's pueblos is mixed. Some families live in the older, hand-built adobe houses, others in mobile homes and modern cinderblock or frame houses built by the Pueblo Tribal Councils. Springing up around the original village, with its dance plazas and kivas, are small neighborhoods and housing developments. Though these may have nicknames like "Desert Storm" or "the Kennedy," they can all be referred to as "the pueblo."

"SAN JUAN CHURCH"
GENNA BUSTOS, AGE 7
WATERCOLOR

LIVING IN A CIRCLE WITH A KIVA IN THE MIDDLE

A pueblo is more than physical buildings and landscape.

"It's living in a circle with a kiva in the middle," says Rose Bean softly. Rose lives with her family near the mouth of Santa Clara Canyon. It's a quiet place, surrounded by plants and animals. According to her mother, Roxanne Swentzell, Rose's words express a keen understanding of Tewa philosophy.

"OUR ROUND KIVA"
EARLE SANCHEZ, AGE 10
WATERCOLOR

"I hope that Rose and her brother Porter will always remember what is important about this place and realize that not everyone lives like this," Roxanne Swentzell tells me. "It's not just that I am related to everybody here, but *I am from here.* I think a lot of people outside of the community don't have a sense of self and place. That's one thing the pueblo can give them: a security in their lives. I look at these hills, these trees, this earth, and I know this is my home."

A Pueblo village makes for a different way of life, one that Victoria Martinez appreciates. "It's fun being here in the summer, being outside playing, going to visit your uncles, your aunts, your friends, and taking walks to the river and riding bikes."

"It's good learning about all the things that took place long ago and going to see old things that are still here," says Heather Dasheno.

Mauricia's words attest to the influence of living with loving grandparents: "I like living here because the older Indian people teach you the ways they lived when they were little. They teach you different kinds of games they played. That's the best part. It's cool being an Indian."

"You have freedom," says Jackie Lopez. "You have your secret hiding places. You can ride your bike almost anywhere without getting hit by a car. Here, we have horses and we're going to get some cows."

"You mainly know everybody, you know most of the old people," says Lydia Martinez.

"Yeah!" says Pam Cata, laughing. "They tell us the right way but we don't listen!"

44

Pam and Lydia are good friends who share a boundless sense of humor. For our interview I am invited to climb a tree in Pam's yard. As we talk about the pueblo, the girls scramble back and forth on the branches and hang upside down by their knees.

"It's a place where Indian people communicate and work together," says Lydia, grabbing for a branch.

". . . as a big family," adds Pam as she dangles from her knees.

That, at least, is the ideal. Like every other community, Pueblo villages have their share of difficulties, such as crime and alcohol abuse.

"I don't like the gangs and the graffiti," says Daniel Archuleta. "They write graffiti on the senior citizens' walls, the houses, and other places. I don't like the disrespect for the elders. That and the yelling outside."

But on the lighter side:

"We don't live by a mall!" exclaims Raelene Gonzales, half serious, half in jest.

"You can't see other people and what they do," says Naomi Naranjo, expressing the sentiments of many young people. "You want to go out and see different attractions, real life."

"You don't get to play baseball, softball, or volleyball with . . . ," Mauricia pauses, then whispers, "white people. Can I say that?"

"Yes."

"With white people," she repeats boldly.

"THE NIGHT SKY"
AMARA GARCIA, AGE 8
OIL PASTEL

"I don't like the way some people treat others here, 'cause I'm light and they're dark," Jackie Lopez says, pointing to her leg.

Many of these children are of mixed descent. The mix might be of pueblos (San Juan and San Felipe), tribes (Pueblo and Navajo), or ethnicity (Pueblo and Spanish, Pueblo and Anglo), or it could be a blend of all of these. Such diversity sometimes leads to family or community problems. At the same time, it can motivate children to explore their Pueblo culture.

"I think having mixed cultures, in many ways, is good because it gives you a chance to learn more about yourself," suggests Melanie Wright. "But I don't think you should have to choose between the cultures. That's probably the hardest thing to do."

45

JULIE VIGIL

PAM CATA (TOP) AND
LYDIA MARTINEZ

ELENA AGUILAR

AUDREY LUJAN

Regardless of the drawbacks, most of the children consider the pueblos a "cool" place to live.

"There's fresh air to breathe," says Daniel.

"It's not as trashy as a city," adds Elena Aguilar. "There's not that many cars."

"There is not a lot of smoke in the air, so you can see clearly," says KhaPovi Harvier. "I like living right by Black Mesa because it's a nice view. If I lived in the city I wouldn't have a backyard to run in, or if I did I'd see another person's house right behind it."

"The pueblo is a lot safer than the city," suggests Shanna Naranjo. "Anywhere you live you're pretty close to one of your friends."

"But you have to be careful at night," Jerome cautions. "My uncle told us that there's people that can turn into dogs. They hide in the bushes by the bridge and grab you." Jerome wonders if we should delete this part of the interview. He's concerned that it might make some kids "a little bit scared" about going out in their own neighborhoods.

Katie sums it up pretty well. "You can do all sorts of things in the pueblo—play in the sand, look for turtles, catch some tadpoles. You can love people, share with them. You can have friends. It's safe. It's fun."

And Naomi reminds one and all of the most important aspect of living in the pueblo: "A pueblo is where your family is."

WHAT DO PUEBLO PEOPLE DO?

Michael "Bucky" Tafoya pops the screen off the kitchen window and slides it open with his hand. "Help her up," he says to me, referring to his younger sister, Tranette. I help Tranette slide through the window so she can open the door for us, since their mom is not home yet.

The door opens and Bucky quickly checks out the house while Tranette heads for the refrigerator and retrieves chocolate cake. We begin our interview seated at the kitchen table. "So, what do Pueblo people do besides break into their own house?" I ask teasingly.

"They dance. They make Pueblo pies, Pueblo cookies, and Pueblo bread." Immediately we are joking.

"Do you drink Pueblo water?"

"Yes," Bucky replies with a giggle, "in a Pueblo house, while sitting at a Pueblo table and watching Pueblo TV!"

Soon Bucky and Tranette's mother, Jessica, arrives with their older sister Gina and baby sister Christina. Gina changes the baby's diaper while Jessica puts groceries away.

"We try to share all the work so that we can have more free time to spend with each other," Jessica says.

MICHAEL TAFOYA

47

Time spent together seems to be a priority in the pueblo. Is it work or is it play? When you're with your family and friends, the boundary between the two tends to blur. "Activity" is a better term to describe much of daily life in a pueblo.

"We get ready for dances and feasts that come up," says Nolan Cruz of San Juan. "The adults work wherever they can find a job. The kids help with chores like washing clothes, cleaning their rooms, vacuuming, taking out the trash, and cutting weeds."

At San Juan Pueblo, the Pacheco sisters and I walk down a long dirt road to the Rio Grande to talk. The riverbank is covered with smooth pebbles and stones. We sit together on a large cottonwood branch and, between bites of vanilla-cream cookies, talk about what Pueblo people do.

"They work!" explains Christine. "In the old days, when the Indians were here, they used to have fields."

"The Indians *are* here," Angela reminds her.

Christine continues: "And every morning they would go out to the fields and take out the weeds and stuff like that."

"Nowadays they have jobs," says Angela.

"Like being a teacher, a secretary, cleaning house, making adobes, and planting a garden," Christine says.

"When they have time in the summer," adds Angela, with an air of authority.

ANGELA AND CHRISTINE PACHECO

I am visiting three young girls at San Ildefonso. We're drawing and talking of many things. Their words are soft as they tell me what Pueblo people do.

"We dance and sing Indian songs," says Larissa Aguilar.

Anything else?

"Yeah," answers her older sister, Elena.

"No," says Raelene Gonzales immediately, hushing her friend.

"Yeah, but I can't tell you," Elena says. "We make Indian food and," she adds in a whisper, "we have doings."

The word "doings" refers to the extensive schedule of ceremonies that take place throughout the Pueblo year. Since they are of a sacred nature, most of these "doings" are not open to the public. Every culture has subjects you just don't talk about with others; for Pueblo kids, this is one of those taboos.

"Most of the people I know make things out of clay, like pots," Rose Bean says. "And they live in trailers and go to fast-food restaurants!" she adds, smiling.

"TREES IN THE CANYON"
KACIE TAFOYA, AGE 6
WATERCOLOR

"WALKING CACTUS"
JACKIE TSOSIE, AGE 11
TEMPERA

There is an endless list of things that make the pueblo a good place to live. But mostly it is the feeling it gives you, one that Juan De La Cruz has found to be simple and true. "It's just that you've known it for many years and have grown up in it. You know it."

JACKIE TSOSIE

JACKIE'S BIKE RIDE

On a warm Saturday afternoon in March, I go for a bicycle ride with a group of children at Santa Clara Pueblo. Blossoming cherry trees border the dirt lane that leads to Jackie Tsosie's house. It was Jackie's suggestion to combine work on this book with a bike ride. With a "Be safe and have fun!" call from Jackie's mother, we take off down the lane toward Shanna Naranjo's house. Across the fields we can see the dense rows of cottonwood trees that line the Rio Grande. The snow-covered Sangre de Cristos loom in the distance.

Shanna, Jackie, and I ride through the quiet pueblo. No one else is out. A few dogs bark. We collect Justin Dasheno at his grandparents' house, then cross the highway to find Jerome Tafoya, out flying his kite. The five of us now ride east from the pueblo and, with much splashing and laughter, cross the Santa Clara Creek where it enters the Rio Grande.

We sit down at the water's edge for a chocolate-chip cookie picnic. Empty beer and pop cans dot the area. But where I see litter, my companions see sport. They set the cans afloat in the river and race along the bank trying to hit them with rocks. Jackie scores twice. She raises both arms over her head and whoops in delight.

Shanna now leads us to "her" beach. As we ride she tells me that she used to come here with her late father, riding her bike beside him while he walked. This landscape holds dear memories. The kids wade in a nearby pond collecting bugs, very aware of the river's power to carry people away in the current. Justin points out his grandpa's fenced field, ready for seeding. During the growing season Justin will spend hours here helping to weed and water corn, squash, and other crops for the fall harvest.

We ride back toward the village through a long grove of cottonwoods. Last year's leaves and twigs crackle beneath our tires. When we get back to the creek, Jackie points out a dozen or more small Christmas trees lying on their sides in the shallow water, their cut-off trunks exposed.

"OLD FRIEND"
JUAN DE LA CRUZ, AGE 12
WATERCOLOR

"This is the Indian way of getting rid of Christmas trees," she says. "It's like 'thank you and good-bye.' They tell us we have to throw our evergreen boughs in the river when we are done dancing, and we do it with our trees, too."

Ever-present is the sense of reciprocity, of returning to and being part of the natural cycle of life. Jackie and I accompany the other children home. We then return to her house with a vow to ride again.

WHAT DOES IT MEAN TO BE PUEBLO?

Riding their bikes past the kiva, participating in family activities, drawing "Indian designs" and other cultural icons—such things fill the children with great personal and community pride. They also help them figure out what it means to be Pueblo.

"What's really fun about being a Pueblo girl is that you can do whatever you want!" says Katie Weahkee.

"Yeah, and it's nice to feel that you belong to a Pueblo and not just a place," says Jackie Lopez.

Daniel Archuleta agrees. "You feel safe most of the time. You know who you are. You know your Indian name. It's dangerous living non-Indian. Of course, it can be dangerous living Indian too, 'cause some people can't get along with each other."

"Being Pueblo means that I get the chance to dance," says Jackie Tsosie. "It makes me feel good to do something in the old tradition."

"Being Pueblo means to believe in your culture and go your Indian ways," begins Mauricia Chavarria.

". . . and learn how to talk your traditional language and respect other cultures and people," adds her sister Danielle Martinez promptly. "If you want to be Indian you have to dance. The only way you can be a true Indian is if you talk the language your people do and . . . finish it off, Bob!" says Danielle, laughing as she thrusts the recorder back to Mauricia.

"It means being proud of what you are," Lydia says.

"And you always go to church on Sunday and try and pray all the nights," admonishes Angela. "And," she adds in a whisper, "we have secret ways and more designs."

"It's just funner being a Pueblo person," confirms Christine.

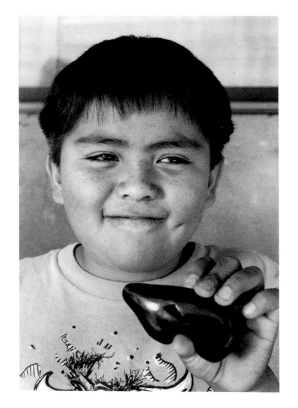

JUSTIN DASHENO

But not always. The encroachment of the larger society on the villages has created an atmosphere of uncertainty. This is a dynamic time, a time when each Pueblo community must decide how best to keep its people in touch with their cultural past while preparing for an unpredictable future. The children are aware of this situation. They too must begin to explore who they are going to be and how they are going to live.

"Well, you're proud of what you are, but you don't have to always be showing it, like wearing a feather in your hair or buckskins and braids," states Julie Vigil. "Like, you look in the encyclopedia under 'Indians' and there'll be someone in buckskins or hardly any clothing. Then if you look in something that's supposed to be up-to-date, it'll show Indian people drunk. Not all Indians are like that, you know. Some are very famous potters and have a lot of money. It's not like all Indians are on welfare." The way Julie tightens her lips and sets her jaw tells me how strongly she feels about this subject.

Pueblo children know they are sometimes viewed as a novelty. That's not a comfortable position for them.

"Around here I'm just another girl from the pueblo," says Naomi. "But when I'm out there I think, 'Oh! I'm an Indian and they'll be asking me questions about stuff.' I think they keep you here in the pueblo too long and then when you go out you think, 'Whoa! Is this what it's like?' Sometimes you want to be Pueblo and sometimes you don't. There's advantages and disadvantages."

One of the great advantages, from a child's perspective, is being part of a community that cares about you and is interested in your well-being. Most adults are willing to take the time to help young people learn and grow.

"They tell you to dance every dance," says Jerome. "They tell you what to do in our Tewa language, where the kiva is, what the river means, to be respectful to it and wash in it before and after you dance. My parents and grandparents say to be respectful to other people, to eat right, and to say thank you when a person gives you something."

"They say to listen to your elders," says Justin, "and take care of your pueblo. If you have Indian stuff you have to take real good care of it. That's the most important thing that you have to do. Take care of your bows and arrows and rattles, and if you have pottery, take care of it too."

Summing up, Lee says simply, "It makes you happy to be Pueblo 'cause you have something special instead of just one certain thing. You have one more culture, one more language, one more everything!"

"CHOPPING WOOD"
JEROME TAFOYA, AGE 7
OIL PASTEL, WATERCOLOR

54

ART LESSON: DRAWING A FAVORITE ACTIVITY

Samantha closes her eyes and imagines the aroma of fresh-baked cookies floating through the air, filling her house with its delicious warmth.

"Yummy!" she says. "They're chocolate chip." She opens her eyes and returns to painting a picture of her aunt carrying a tray of cookies from the oven.

I had asked Samantha's class of second-graders to draw a favorite family activity. A look around the classroom reveals a variety of scenes: making pottery, riding bikes, chopping wood. "Put as many details in the large object as you can," I instruct. Buttons, aprons, eyelashes, and other things appear.

The children have also been studying their favorite picture books to see how professional artists create the illusion of depth. Depth is the feeling of near and far in a picture. One way to create it is to vary the size of objects. Big things appear closer and small things look farther away.

"Look, Bruce! My auntie is so close I can get a cookie!"

DO IT!

Think of an activity that you or someone in your family enjoys doing. Draw the person performing that activity so that they reach from top to bottom on the paper. Drawing something big makes it appear important and close. Look carefully at how the person looks. What expression is shown? Is she holding anything? What is he wearing? Draw in all the possible details.

Now work on the background, making the objects small so they will look far away. Where is this person? What is behind her? Finally, color in the whole picture.

"MY AUNT MAKING COOKIES"
SAMANTHA BACA, AGE 7
WATERCOLOR

55

"THE THREE INDIANS ARE DANCING"
SHERRIE CATANACH, AGE 6
OIL PASTEL, WATERCOLOR

Put a Little Color in Your Mind

T HE KIVA!" SHOUT THE CHILDREN of San Ildefonso Day School enthusiastically when I ask what they would like to draw or paint. The round kiva of the south plaza has become an icon that attracts many artists, both Pueblo and non-Pueblo. "It's our kiva," the children say with pride.

Kivas symbolize Pueblo culture to the outside world, representing a way of life not always understood or appreciated. Every pueblo has at least two kivas, or ceremonial chambers, one for the Winter people and one for the Summer people. Each Pueblo member belongs to one kiva or the other.

These sacred spaces function as the heart of the pueblo. Their silent presence is a daily reminder of how to live one's life. For young minds, kivas are also an excellent inspiration for drawing and for divergent thinking. There may be only one round kiva at San I, but a multitude of angles, colors, and textures can be used to paint or draw it.

On this particular day the children's visions range from realistic watercolors by Earle, Angelina, and Sam to Lee's fanciful painting of a dog "flying" in front of the kiva while an elder ascends the ladder. Using oil pastels and black paper, Mark and Raelene create marvelous shapes and colors. The kiva, or anything else for that matter, need not be depicted as the color it is—not when there are so many colors to choose from and blend together! The children's finished artwork reflects their individual personalities. At the same time, their focused concentration connects them ever more strongly to their culture.

WAYNE VIGIL

Architecture is a "safe" subject for these young artists. Some cultural images are not. There are numerous signs and symbols that are reserved solely for religious purposes and may not be replicated for any other use. These include representations of katsinas, the spirit beings who guard over Pueblo life. Other images, like the Sun Face, geometric designs, and stylized animals and pottery forms, are reproduced in a wide variety of settings. What is permissible varies by pueblo, kiva association, and family. Drawing Pueblo subjects motivates children to learn more about and identify with their culture. It is also an opportunity for elders to instruct children in the distinction between the sacred and the secular.

"AFTER FIRING"
KIMBERLY GARCIA, AGE 11
COLORED PENCIL

SOURCES OF PUEBLO DESIGN

Drawing, painting, and working with clay put children inside a cycle of expression that has existed among Pueblo people for more than a thousand years. Most of the forms and images of contemporary Pueblo art derive from those used in the past, and those images themselves emerged directly from the immediate environment. People did, and still do, "live in the earth." Homes, ovens, and kivas are still made from earthen materials. Stylized representations of clouds, lightning, mountains, animals, and other designs permeate the Pueblo world. The children identify closely with them. They know them to be theirs.

"We get the designs we draw from our ancestors, from petroglyphs and pieces of broken pottery from a long time ago," says KhaPovi Harvier. "They're different from a regular animal, object, or living person. The shapes, sizes, and mythical tales make them different. They might have a swirl for a body instead of an oval form with fur or scales on it."

"The reason I draw the designs is to make the past and present come together," adds her brother, Jordan. "It's like mixing colors."

"When I walk through the pueblo I see different designs, like in the church and on the houses and the walls and the kiva steps," says Mauricia Chavarria. "My style is Indian designs because that's what I see most of wherever I go. I've got them stored in my head. When I go somewhere else, like to a museum, I find different designs and I keep them in my head until I get home. Then I put them together and I have a picture!"

THE POTTERY TRADITION

Pottery making, the most prominent traditional Pueblo art form, connects the potters and their families to the land in a unique way. Clay is not purchased; it comes from the Clay Mother, the spirit of the earth, who is also the source of the talent that enables potters to provide for their families. Before digging, a good potter will pray to the Clay Mother, sprinkle cornmeal as a blessing, and then remove only as much clay as is needed. If this is done, the Clay Mother will replenish the clay and keep the potter and her family supplied for generations. Greedy potters, however, may end up with nothing.

Preparing to make pottery requires a great deal of physical work. The clay must be processed, screened, soaked, screened again, and dried. Wood or manure must be gathered for the firing. A potter will talk to the clay and form it to the shape it wants to be. The shaped object is then carved, polished, or painted. Another prayer is said when it is put into the oven for firing. The finished pieces are not only beautiful; they also represent a way of living in which family is of primary importance.

POTTERY BY ELIZA MORSE, KHAPOVI HARVIER, VICTORIA MARTINEZ, MICHAEL TAFOYA (CLOCKWISE FROM TOP LEFT)

THE GONZALES BOYS

Because working in clay is family work, many Tewa children are clay artists themselves. Probably the best-known Pueblo potter is Maria Martinez of San Ildefonso. Working with her husband, Julian, she is credited with revitalizing Pueblo pottery in the 1920s and lifting it to the status of fine art. Today her black-on-black style is practiced by many potters. The Gonzales brothers—Brandan, age 11, and Derek, age 8—have learned how to work with the clay from their mother, Barbara. When you watch their nimble fingers you can see generations at work. Brandan and Derek are great-great-grandsons of the famed Maria.

"I think of her whenever I make pottery," says Derek. "I picture her making pottery. She helps me when I'm thinking of her."

BRANDAN AND DEREK
GONZALES

MICHAEL TAFOYA

"I wish she was still living so she could teach me to do bigger pottery," adds Brandan.

"That would be cool," responds Derek.

The Gonzales brothers make pottery at home as well as at their mother's Sunbeam pottery studio and snack bar. Small clusters of local children lay down their bicycles and enter the store to buy candy bars, soda pops, or pickles. Brandan sucks on a juicy pickle and talks about pottery.

"I make on-tu, which are moccasins, plates, little ovens, bowls, and necklaces," he says. "I used to do dinosaurs when I was about three or four years old. I got the idea from the movie *Jurassic Park*. People liked them, but I don't make them anymore. It was time to move on."

"I started when I was three," says Derek as he forms a clay sculpture of Black Mesa, the large, dark landform that overlooks San Ildefonso. "I didn't like it at first 'cause I'd never touched clay, but then when it dried on my hands I liked it. What I like best about making pottery is when it dries on your fingers. It feels like you got stuck in a puddle of concrete."

"We spend about thirty or sixty minutes a day making pottery," Brandan and Derek tell me.

"Once I get them to sit down," Barbara Gonzales interjects with a chuckle.

"We make one to three pieces a day in the summer. If we're really bored we make more. Mom rolls the clay into certain size balls. Then we make the pottery," they say.

These are boys, regular kids. Pottery making vies for their time with baseball, basketball, getting wet in the sprinklers, video games, and TV. It's one of many activities they enjoy.

I ask their mother what she feels her job is. Before she can answer, Derek says, "She's our role model."

"And inspiration!" adds his mother, laughing.

MICHAEL TAFOYA

"I like squishing the clay into a turtle," says Michael Tafoya. Under his mother's guidance Michael and his sisters and cousins are learning to make pottery. "I mostly make animals like turtles, bears, and sometimes little bowls. I've learned to respect the clay just like I respect my parents and grandparents."

"It's like this," says his mother, Jessica. "Mother Earth gives to us, and we respect her for giving us a way of living. Our pottery is a family tradition. We carry it on from one generation to the next."

"I carry on my family's tradition by reusing my grandmother's designs," adds Michael.

Pueblo potters regard traditional designs as gifts from the ancestors. These designs are carried on through the generations with a great deal of respect. Each new hand that works a gifted design is touching the past while it infuses the design with the energy and creative ideas of the present.

Michael sits at a table with his mother, his sister Gina, and his cousin Melanie. A few of the younger girls weave in and out of the kitchen, watching and asking if they can help. They are given clay. Grandpa hauls in groceries. An uncle brings in new clothes for the littlest children. There is joking and news of the day. It is clear that the family that clays together stays together.

WAYNE AND CELESTINO YAZZA

Families also pay bills together. Brothers Wayne and Celestino Yazza contribute to their family's economic well-being by making pottery. "If we don't do clay we don't eat or go anywhere," says Wayne.

"We pay our electric bills and propane with the money we earn," says Celestino. "And we buy our school supplies and dance outfits."

The two boys work in clays that reflect their dual ancestry: their mother's red Santa Clara clay and the sparkling micaceous clay of their father's Picuris Pueblo.

"It's soggy," says Wayne with a quiet smile. In his hand is a ball of wet clay that oozes through his fingers as he squeezes.

"You can get a lot of money just for selling one," adds Celestino. "People say, 'You have nice work,' and then you say, 'Thank you.'"

"We treat the clay like it's our brother or sister or mom," says Wayne with certainty. The tone of his voice indicates he is not saying this lightly. "It's not like a toy," he adds. "The Great Spirit gives us our money, our life, our food. It comes down through the pottery."

"We respect pottery," says Celestino.

"The clay is our life," they say together.

CELESTINO AND WAYNE YAZZA

"MAKING POTTERY"
ROBYN MARTINEZ, AGE 11
COLORED PENCIL

ROSE BEAN

ROSE BEAN

Rose Bean comes from a family of clay artists. Her great-grandmother, also named Rose, taught all of her children to work in clay. Some still work in traditional forms. Others, like Nora Naranjo-Morse, Rose's aunt, make figures and videos with a Pueblo voice. Michael Naranjo, her uncle, is a well-known sculptor. Rose's mother, Roxanne Swentzell, has taken the figure in new directions, making faces and bodies that are so realistic you are convinced they will dance or gossip once you leave the workroom. Growing up in such a diverse and creative family, it is no wonder that Rose, too, has gone in her own direction.

"I've made animals and people and all sorts of things," says Rose. "I really like tiny things. Tiny little ovens, tiny little frying pans, tiny little forks and spoons, tiny rugs, tiny chairs. Now I make clay dolls. I make the clothes for them on Mama's treadle sewing machine."

Rose leads an independent life. She and her older brother are home-taught and live in an adobe building designed and constructed by their mother and friends without a blueprint. Organic, self-sustaining farming is practiced outside the house. Inside, hand-made tools and furniture accentuate the simple, spacious living space. Anywhere else the Swentzell's style of living would be considered "alternative," but here, on a sunny June day, it just seems to make common sense.

"I think my life is a lot different than a lot of other kids' lives. My cousin Devonna has computer games and all kinds of things like that. I don't. We don't even have electricity! Most kids have the TV constantly playing. They don't ever get to take care of plants and chickens, turkeys and sheep."

Rose's lifestyle recognizes no boundaries between making art and living life. Learning clay is a lifelong process that begins at home.

"I learn by watching Mama, just watching," Rose tells me. "I like forming things with my fingers. It's easier to get three dimensions with clay than with drawing. And it tastes good!"

A taste for clay is not restricted to children. Pueblo people of all generations have told me stories about eating clay, and pregnant women are said to have a special craving for it. "Clay establishes unity," Judy Harvier says. "Many of us eat it and so we are bound together by the clay."

"I used to like to eat the clay," says KhaPovi Harvier. "It tasted good. One time I thought it looked like a thin cake with chocolate frosting on it. That's how it looks when my dad spreads it out to dry. So I got some of what I thought was frosting and I ate it. I thought dirt got in the frosting. I tried another section and it tasted the same. I thought that my mom left it out by mistake and that dust came through the front door and got on it." She laughs at the memory.

"I made my first pottery when I was six or seven years old," KhaPovi goes on. "I learned from my dad and his mother. When you work with clay you treat it like—what's that phrase? Do unto it like you'd like done to you. Which means treat it with respect, don't beat it up, don't waste it, and make something you like with it."

Tewa children come from families who feel a kinship with the earth.

"The clay has provided most everything for us," says KhaPovi's father, Andrew Harvier. "The Clay Mother has been very good to us. Once upon a time we were heavily involved in the mainstream society, working in professional careers. The clay has allowed us to return home, to be with each other, and raise our children."

Judy Harvier adds, "Our 'family' grows as our pottery art, our 'babies,' reach out into the four corners of the world carrying with them our messages of peace, harmony, and unity. Our collectors become sharers of our beliefs. We have become one in heart, mind, and spirit, heading in the same direction. We are traveling a beautiful path together."

HISTORIC PUEBLO PAINTING

According to art historian J. J. Brody, modern Pueblo painting began in 1909 when a teacher at San Ildefonso Day School handed out art supplies and had her students paint whatever they wanted. They painted winter dances. Today, Pueblo children up and down the Rio Grande make dynamic visual images out of a rich and diverse "art" environment highlighted by dance, song, and the making of pottery.

"It's more challenging to draw in the traditional style," Naomi Naranjo says. "There's more detail, so I have to concentrate more."

Those early days nurtured a number of artists who pioneered the incorporation of two-dimensional art in the Pueblo concept of creativity. Among them were Pablita Velarde, Tony Da, Awa Tsireh, Geronima Montoya, and J. D. Roybal. These elder painters are known to many of the kids simply as grandma, grandpa, and great-grandma.

"My great-aunt, Pablita Velarde, painted a picture of my dad dancing the Corn Dance," says Jackie Tsosie. "I like her pictures because they have a lot of color. She used to tell me to draw as much as possible. I hope someday I will be a painter like her."

KHAPOVI HARVIER

"BASKET DANCER"
NAOMI NARANJO, AGE 12
TEMPERA

"FIVE BROTHERS"
JORDAN HARVIER, AGE 12
COLORED PENCIL

SHANNA NARANJO

TRICIA DASHENO

HEATHER DASHENO

WHERE DO IDEAS COME FROM?

The landscape in which we grow up forms, informs, and determines the patterns of our individual lives and the basic visual expressions of our various cultures. Throughout the world, human life comprises similar elements. There are birth, development, family, food, work, shelter, clothing, language and other forms of communication and expression, relationship to nature, aging, death. Where these elements occur plays a large part in what makes us different. The natural forms of northern New Mexico have brought forth a unique array of designs and patterns from the Tewa people and, from their children, a unique understanding of the creative process.

"My ideas come from my subconscious," says Shanna Naranjo. She lives at the eastern edge of Santa Clara Pueblo with her mother and little sister. Talented in many areas, Shanna has a special fondness for original thinking. "Sometimes I record things that I see or hear and put them together. They are typed into my mind. They come out when I want to put something else in. Like, my mind will fill up, and then I'll see something and it'll start going in and then my thoughts come out. When new ideas go in, the old thoughts come out, and that's when it's time to draw."

"Most of my ideas come from my head and some of them I just doodle and it comes out to a masterpiece!" claims a confident Daniel Archuleta. "I close my eyes and I see the finished picture in my head and it's colored and everything and I just put it down. When I think about it, it happens on the paper. I just look at it very clearly and figure out what else I can put into it and then it comes out to whatever I think of."

For other children the answer to the question of where ideas come from is simpler.

"My head, *duh!*" exclaims Devonna Naranjo. "I think about 'em. There are still pictures . . . in my head."

"My ideas come from the colors," adds Elena Aguilar. "And from my imagination. I just put my brush on the paper and away it goes!"

"I get ideas from books," says Tricia Dasheno. "I look at pictures, learn about them, read about them, then I draw it. You keep looking at it and looking at it and then it pops out of your brain!"

"And that's where you get your main ideas," adds her cousin Justin.

"Just put a little color into your mind," suggests Heather, "and think of how it will look when it's all together. And if you like it the way you're thinking about it you just start putting it on paper."

"My head, my head, my head," say Katie Weahkee and Natanni and Paige Mirabal in unison: "Like, like, like . . . "

"Like if I think of a jungle I'll draw," says Katie, taking command of the question. "It shows up in my head like a picture. I get a little bit done and I do the rest, piece by piece."

"Like from my dad," adds Natanni. "He does sculptures. Lions, horses, eagles, buffaloes, bears, deer, elk . . . the world."

"Like from God?" Paige wonders. "It moves onto the paper. It moves through your arm when you're painting."

"I just think of some things that I haven't done since I was little," says Jackie Tsosie, "like playing baseball and going fishing. All my pictures come from all the nature I see."

"I just think when my grandma tells me about the olden days and I ask her some weird questions," says Lee Moquino. "A lot of things go through my mind. I just sit and think for like five minutes and then something comes into my head. It's like a picture. You can see it. It's all done. I look at everything first and make it on the paper."

Jerome Tafoya is as comfortable creating detailed pencil drawings as he is making free-flowing monotypes. For him the process is clear and easily accessible.

"I get ideas from my imagination. If it comes out a little bit but I can't see the whole picture in my imagination, then I just remember another detail and add on to it. Let me close my eyes and see." Jerome remains quiet for a while. The relaxed smile on his face tells me he's having fun with this idea, roaming the inside of his head. Opening his eyes he says, "When I imagine a drawing I just draw it on a piece of paper and then I think of something else and just add it on. When I make a mistake I just fix it into something else."

JEROME TAFOYA

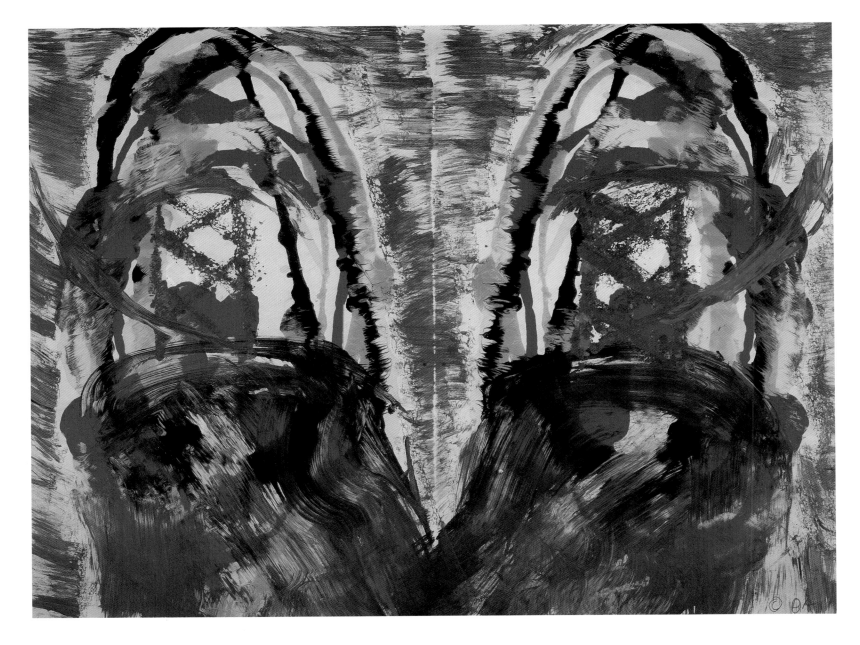

"RAINBOW MOCCASINS"
DANIEL ARCHULETA, AGE 12
TEMPERA

70

Mistakes, or more precisely the fear and perception of mistakes, are one of the greatest obstacles in making art with children. Many young artists judge their work too soon and therefore feel disappointed. They want everything to be just so, and usually that "just so" is the way a professional commercial image looks. Having the playful confidence to keep working at an idea, to change it and let it change your thinking, is a valuable life skill that all of us can cultivate. What do you do when you're stuck, can't find an idea, or decide you've made a "mistake"?

"I'd say close your eyes and think in your mind, or look outside and draw something that's outside," Jerome suggests. "I would tell them to fix it up a little, add a little detail."

"I would start them off a little bit," says Angela Pacheco. "I'd tell them what to draw and then they can draw it. Or if they say, 'I don't want to draw that,' then I would say, 'You can draw whatever you want.'"

"They could do half and I would do half," adds Christine.

"I'd say look at that girl's T-shirt over there!" laughs Julie Vigil.

"Julie, check your batteries," responds her friend Audrey Lujan.

"You have to have a feel for it," says Juan De La Cruz. "You have to know what you're going to draw before you start on it." This twelve-year-old is as committed to his computer and school studies as he is to drawing. He approaches all of his work with a great deal of confidence and eagerness to learn. "Think of your favorite subject, draw that, and add on to it as you go along."

"I would tell 'em to look in all kinds of books," suggests Tricia. In her characteristic mischievous fashion she adds, "Look at pots, look at pans, look at pillows, look at blankets"—here she starts to giggle—"look at baskets, look outside at what you see, *aaaaannnnnd*, that's it."

SOURCES OF IMAGINATION

Pueblo designs and patterns permeate the children's ideas of art, as natural to them as rainbows, Mickey Mouse, and sun-in-the-corner landscapes are to other children. But what ultimately appears on the page is influenced by a variety of forces.

"I draw or paint when I'm mad or bored," declares Jackie Lopez with a grin of self-awareness. "I show my feelings on the paper. I get mad enough to draw when I can't go somewhere, or if I can't do something or I can't get my way!" She laughs. "I draw everything mad. My stuffed animals—mad; me—mad; my mom saying, 'Get to your room!'; and my TV—mad. Everything has a mad face on it. When I get happy I throw them away."

"I just grew up with it," says Nolan. "My dad's an artist. I watched him when I was a little kid."

JORDAN HARVIER

"Well, I kinda taught myself," says Devonna with a sheepish smile beginning on her face. "When I was a kid? When I was four? I scribbled on the wall. A lot!"

"Man, did she!" exclaims her mother, Teresa.

"And then I watched Rosie, I watched my dad, I watched my mom, I watched other people, and then I learned how."

"I draw when I have nothing to do," offers Jackie Tsosie. "Sometimes I get an idea from something that I see showing on TV. Or when I look through books I get an idea of what to draw. Then I get my art kit and my paper, sit at the table, and go to work."

"When you draw it's like you can tell a story," says Jerome. "One time I was at my p'óp'oejiyás' [godparents'] home and I drew a buffalo dancer for my godmother, Seta. I didn't want her to see it so I hid it when she came close. She fell asleep. When my parents came to pick me up I put the picture by her head. Then we left. She saw it when she woke up the next day. Kind of like Santa Claus!"

Jerome is a dedicated artist who draws all the time. Sometimes he can be found still drawing at his desk after everyone else has gone to lunch. How many eight-year-olds do you know who are willing to forego recess in order to finish a drawing? Jerome is that kid, and he is as dedicated to his other subjects as he is to art.

"And you get to get dirty!" exclaims Elena joyfully. "It just makes you feel good!"

Along with a healthy community and a caring home, other elements may be required before art can be created. "When I do art I sit inside in a cool place, with something that smells good, like food cooking. My mom's chicken and corn tortillas give me spectacular ideas that I never thought of before," jokes Jordan Harvier. "It's like I'm a car that needs gas. When I get filled up I run better!"

His sister, KhaPovi, has a different approach. "I like a clean table with no junk on it, just my art supplies. I like to have a little drink by me. I like listening to the TV while I'm doing my work because they say different words on there and I try to draw what they're explaining."

"You have to have music—rap," says Elena.

"Ninety-seven point three," adds Raelene, specifying her favorite radio station. "And I have to be by myself."

"I'm usually sitting on my bed with my art pad in front of me and eating chips and sometimes I have music on—The Eagles, or Tina Turner," says Shanna. "I might just lay there for a little while until the idea comes to me. Then I sit up and think about how I'm going to draw it. I'll start drawing with a pencil and probably color it in."

"I have to have a picture or something, and base it on that," says Juan. "It's usually quiet unless somebody is watching TV. I spend more time at home doing my pictures than in school, so I get way detailed. In school you only have thirty minutes or something. But at home I spend hours on it."

"I like to be outside," states Naomi. "I can't draw from inside, 'cause it's like too closed in. I have to be where it's open. You can see better and you can imagine how it will be."

"Sometimes when I feel like drawing I put on an Indian tape," says Victoria Martinez. "My favorite is Red Thunder. It gets me relaxed and then I draw."

"What I like to have around is paper, scissors, paint, pencils, Justin, Josh, my little sister Alex, and my parents, Rosita and Walter," says Tricia without taking a breath. "They're artists, too. Also chile, carrots, sweet potatoes, broccoli, soup and salad, and ice cream. Coke, candy, beer—I'm just kidding—and milk, rice, apples, tomatoes, and bananas. Mainly bananas."

"CRAZY NORA TURTLE"
CHRISTINE PACHECO, AGE 6
OIL PASTEL, WATERCOLOR

Katie contributes her list: "TV, Mom and Dad, people, rocks, paper, water, a soft drink. I work on the kitchen table. I get my ideas from my dad. If he's drawing a river or a lake, say, I use a part of that and start drawing my picture."

Facing the sky, Paige directs her comments there, as if she is talking to the entire universe. "I like to have people around," she announces. "I like to have my mom and dad, my brother and sister. I like to have Katie and my grandma and grandpa. I like to have sculptures around the studio." She stops abruptly and nods her head to signify that she's done.

"We're mainly in her room," says Pam Cata, nodding to her friend Lydia Martinez, "with the window open, birds chirping . . . "

"People yelling," adds Lydia.

"With the radio loud . . . "

"We usually have Kool-Aid in a bag that we suck on," concludes Lydia.

"My family and I are sitting in the living room," says Nathana Bird. "I draw on the coffee table in the living room. I always have the TV on all the time when I draw. I always have Kool-Aid, too."

"I don't care what's around me," says Devonna. "I can pretty much draw anywhere."

CAMI LEA PORTER

CAMI'S CONFIDENCE

Making art is like learning a language. There are skills and techniques to master, or at least get acquainted with. Shapes and colors are like words and sentences that you use to communicate. Underlying everything are themes of self-esteem, exploration, and confidence. Confidence is what Cami Lea Porter is all about.

"My heart tells me that I have confidence and I could make my confidence bigger," she says.

I met Cami through the Eight Northern Indian Pueblos Visitor Guide, where her small advertisement was tucked among the names of well-known artists and galleries. I wanted to meet the girl who had enough confidence to place such an ad.

"Well, I was looking in a magazine and saw how some people put ads in," Cami explained. "I asked, 'Mom, Dad. Can I put an ad in?' They said, 'Sure!' And then I had to make some money to pay for it.

"I got started in art by messing around with paint. I'd bring my stuff home from school and my mom would say, 'That's really good! You could sell your paintings and save money for college.'

"To make good art you have to have confidence," Cami says. "You have to believe in yourself, you have to know what you're going to do, and if you have the power.

"I mostly paint the traditions that I have, like the pueblo and my culture. To draw I just look at certain things, study them. I don't really think it in my head, I just do it. My brain tells me to move to the left, move to the right. When I get stuck I look through books. I see designs and do something similar to that."

Cami lives near the village of Nambé with her parents, older sister, and two brothers. From their front door you can see the snowy tops of the nearby Sangre de Cristo Mountains. Open land surrounding the house gives Cami a big yard to play in and a great sense of what it is to be Pueblo.

"To be Pueblo means life. It means freedom. And it means to be somebody I am. I get to dance. I get to do things that other people don't get to do in life. I feel like I'm free. I'm not trapped in a city. Living here you can run around screaming, you can jump rope, you can wander off on nature walks. I usually go down where the horses are, feed them, pet them, and walk in the fields. I go to where the cottonwood trees are and find a little spot and make that my hiding place. I think about the next day, or how it would be if I was alone and didn't have any family and I was in the wild and I was an animal. I like to sit down under a tree and watch the birds fly. I like to go chasing the quails around in the field and try to catch one. I like looking for weird-shaped rocks."

Placing an ad and attending to all the tasks attached to it is a big job for an eleven-year-old. Turning "pro" requires learning about responsibility, economics, and yourself.

"You have to put hard work in to sell it. You have to think, How long did this painting take, how much effort did I put into it? You have to add up all that stuff and then you put a price on it. I do one painting at a time. If I don't like it then I have to fix it up 'cause I'm not going to go wasting good paper. It's expensive!"

When I ask Cami for business advice, she smiles and replies, "Do what you want to. I did it, and I made a big effort. It's something I did with my life. Just do it!"

TO MAKE GOOD ART YOU HAVE TO . . .

In the right environment, work and play can mean the same thing. Making good art is both work and play, and other things as well. A survey of the children reveals that to make good art you have to:

"Really think about it," replies Juan without a moment's hesitation.

"Have a good imagination and think of your favorite things, what you like to do," offers Victoria.

"It starts out when your brain shoots a message to your arm and your hand and you start doing drawing," says Julie.

"MY BROTHER'S STRIPES"
CAMI LEA PORTER, AGE 10
WATERCOLOR ON CANVAS

"You have to believe in yourself and get what's stored in your mind out, so you can store more," Mauricia suggests. "You have to be original by thinking of your own designs and not copying any designs that have already been used."

"Just put your mind to it," states Lee clearly. "Whatever you're making, don't go all crazy and scribble all over your paper. You've got to really think of what you're doing and concentrate on every little mark. I learn about what I'm thinking when I do art."

"You have to be yourself, calm, relaxed. Just draw everything that comes to you and, like writing, you can edit it," suggests Jordan.

"Use your imagination," says Devonna. "You have to be into the attitude of wanting to draw."

"Put all your work into it and try hard to make the best art you can," adds Heather.

Making art is a personal conversation between artist, materials, and ideas. Five-year-old Paige Mirabal knows this and, with a single word, reminds us all:

"Listen."

"COYOTE"
QUINCY TAFOYA, AGE 12
LATEX AND WOOD

76

ART LESSON: USING RADIAL DESIGN TO ORGANIZE IMAGES

Do you ever have so many design ideas that you can't squeeze them into one drawing? Mauricia does. She studies and collects Indian designs and patterns by riding her bike through the pueblo.

Radial designs are found in cultures around the world and range from Tibetan mandalas to Navajo sandpaintings. The format provides children with a comfortable structure. The repetition of imagery creates a sense of motion and has plenty of diverse options, so that no two designs will be the same. The radial design form provided Mauricia with a wonderful new way to express her creativity.

"There's no top or bottom to it," she says. "It just keeps moving around and around!"

DO IT!

The trickiest part of creating a radial design is constructing the basic framework of lines. Find the center of a square piece of paper by drawing diagonal lines lightly from corner to opposite corner. Next, using a ruler, find the halfway points of each side and connect them with lines that go through the center of the paper. These lines will serve as your guide to making your own design. You can divide the paper further by drawing lines to make geometric or other shapes.

Radial designs are meant to repeat. Every time you draw something in one section of your paper, be sure to draw it in the opposite section. It is usually good to draw two or four of everything. You can simply use line designs or draw your favorite objects, or combine the two. And what if you don't know what to draw? All good artists draw from their experiences and immediate environments. Look around you! Toys, cars, dolls, tools, food, and nature are all good sources of inspiration.

"LOOKING INTO THE WORLD OF SYMBOLS"
MAURICIA CHAVARRIA, AGE 12
COLORED PENCIL

"DANCING TABLITAS"
GINA CHAVARRIA, AGE 11
OIL PASTEL, WATERCOLOR

Dancing to Get a Good Heart

DEER DANCE, SAN JUAN

I T IS A WARM EVENING, the twelfth of August, a few years ago. Eight-year-old KhaPovi Harvier and her brother, Jordan, age ten, have just spent the entire day dancing in honor of the Santa Clara Pueblo Feast Day. It was the first time the children participated in the dance.

KhaPovi hugs her mother and speaks to her in Tewa, bestowing upon her a special blessing. Jordan follows. KhaPovi then walks toward her father, her steps heavy with fatigue. She offers the same blessing to him. "May your life be long!" is the blessing given from child to adult, man to woman, woman to man, and dancers to family members when they return home after dancing. The sun sets on the distant mountains, turning their peaks golden. Rain-bearing clouds linger. In the shadow of this special day KhaPovi's eyes are droopy, her brow sweaty; yet her smile is bright with a new understanding of herself and her people.

THE PUEBLO DANCES

Corn. Buffalo. Deer. Comanche. Cloud. Turtle. These are some of the names given to the colorful, rhythmic dances performed by the Tewa-speaking Pueblos of northern New Mexico. Although the public is welcome on feast days, the activities are not a spectacle put on for tourists. They are part of a year-round, continuing cycle of ceremony through which the people show their respect for the forces of nature and the spirits that control them. These rituals must be performed to maintain a balance between natural and spiritual powers. Through them, the spirits give the people the things they need to survive.

79

COMANCHE DANCE, SAN
ILDEFONSO (NORTH SIDE)

"The purpose of dancing is to get a good heart," says Lee Moquino, "and for everything to be good. When you dance you pray for those things and you live longer."

"It's to give the animals respect from our people," says Christine Pacheco.

"And so the spirit can come down and see them and so he can bless them and their clothes . . . I mean their Indian jewelry," adds her sister, Angela.

"And you can dance for a special person when they die," states Daniel Archuleta quietly. "December 26 is the Turtle. That's when my father was born. I dance the Turtle Dance at San Juan every year to remember him. Another reason is to respect the spirits. The Eagle Dance is to show the great respect we have for that creature."

"It's like going to church and asking God for help," says Naomi Naranjo. "But in a way you have to participate to ask for your own. If you dance you get more help. You also ask for blessings for other people."

Pueblo feast day dances offer the community and visitors the opportunity to acknowledge and participate in the total integration of human life with nature. Dance, song, drum, prayer, colorful and symbolic dress, people-watching, the sharing of food, reciprocity, the circle of life—all these separate elements come together in a celebration of humanity.

Feast days are held in each pueblo once a year on the days honoring the patron saint of that particular pueblo. San Ildefonso's Feast Day is January 22 and 23. Few visitors brave the frost-tinged dawn to watch the Deer dancers enter the plaza. San Juan's is June 23 and 24, and offers a carnival for the children. It is usually crowded and hot. Nambé celebrates St. Francis of Assisi Feast Day on October 3 and 4. Te Tsu Geh honors San Diego on November 12. Guadalupe Feast Day is held at Pojoaque on December 12. At each pueblo the celebration is highlighted by vespers, mass, dancing, and a sharing of food in family homes, all contributing to the experience of communing with the elements responsible for life.

The interpretation of a particular dance varies from pueblo to pueblo, kiva to kiva, and year to year. The Deer Dance performed at San Juan is different from the one at San Ildefonso. Within a pueblo, different dances are performed by each kiva group. In Santa Clara, for instance, as many as four separate groups can be dancing and drumming at once in the various dance areas.

The dances chosen change with the season. Deer, Buffalo, and Antelope are performed in the winter so that the taking of animals during a hunt will not be offensive to the spirits. The Cloud Dance is held in the spring to request nature's assistance in growing crops. The Corn Dance and other dances held in the fall ask for a good harvest. The Comanche Dance, in which male participants dress in Plains Indian attire, can be performed year-round. Each dance also symbolizes the people's connection to their ancestors.

"They all bring something good to our pueblo," says Danielle Martinez. "Rain to water our plants. We do the Harvest for our crops. We usually do the Deer in the winter time. Everybody goes hunting in the fall, so we thank the spirits for all the deer we've caught."

"The deer are very special to us 'cause they are like *our* animals," emphasizes Jackie Lopez. "They are animals that we depend on."

"Some of the people dance to make them feel better about some things that go wrong in the pueblo," says Jackie Tsosie. "I dance to feel good about things I want to do, like helping my relatives who live far away. I think about them while I am dancing."

"It's to bring back what was once done. It's important 'cause if the dances are not done, then they will be lost," states Julie Vigil.

"We dance for the culture," says Katie Weahkee. "You get to learn things you didn't know, like how to use a fan. We dance to pray for Nature, to give thanks for all the things she has done for us . . . rain, snow, she keeps us warm, and all that. It's for the deer and all the other kinds of animals. She lets us kill them, but we have to use every piece of them. She made us. She made the world, and that's all."

"DEER DANCER"
EARLE SANCHEZ, AGE 10
TEMPERA

82

"DEER DANCE"
MARK CATA, AGE 8
WATERCOLOR

PREPARING TO DANCE

For the young child dancing for the first time, the dance is an important step along the path of knowing what it is to be Pueblo.

KhaPovi and Jordan Harvier have chosen to dance this year for the first time. Today they will dance the Corn at Santa Clara Pueblo. Their decision is significant in many ways. First, it concerns the question of how culture is transferred from one generation to the next in a quickly changing society.

"I just wanted to feel what it was like to dance," says Jordan with his customary easy-going smile when asked what prompted his decision.

"I thought it would be fun!" adds KhaPovi. "I asked my parents. They said, 'Are you sure?' and I said, 'Yes, I'm sure.'"

To the children, the first dance means commitment, practicing, experiencing the kiva and its rules for the first time, peaked emotions, nervous excitement, and fun. To the family, it means supporting the child's commitment by assembling the dance outfit, preparing food to serve on Feast Day, and conducting a giveaway.

WAYNE AND CELESTINO YAZZA,
HARVEST DANCE, SANTA CLARA

"When they first said they wanted to dance, it was like a rock dropping on us, but in a good way," says Judy Harvier with a smile. "The decision should be theirs," she continues. "My children started learning to dance before they were born. When I was pregnant, and then when they were infants, we took them to dances, on trips, everywhere. When Jordan was small he would play dancing but would never volunteer at school. KhaPovi would always volunteer for dances at school, but neither of them voiced an interest in Feast Day until this year. We just let it happen. I don't like being forced either, so I didn't want to force my kids to do something like this, something that's sacred."

"When I first danced we were coaxed by being told, 'This is for the people, but you'll get all these gifts, too, and maybe some money,'" says Andrew, KhaPovi and Jordan's father. "Some children would probably prefer not to dance, and some are not given a choice, but I'll tell you something. No matter what led you to dance, when you first put your foot down to dance, you enjoy it. Any reluctance you may have disappears instantly, especially when people come up to you and say, 'You danced so well.' It's a big charge!"

83

Preparations for a dance often begin months in advance. There are many items to be gathered, many questions to be answered.

"Immediately I had a huge list in my mind of things to get for their clothing," sighs Judy. "The rest is easy, the food, and help from the family."

"The big thing for me is to maintain their motivation," says Andrew, "They were sincere when they asked and we said yes, but that was months ago. We keep them interested by keeping them involved. And then there are the questions."

"What happens in the kiva, Dad?"

"What am I going to do without any moccasins?"

"Can I paint the tablita?"

"They constantly ask to help," says Andrew. "They plead to become involved in the whole event, to become an important and noticeable part of the family and community."

Both children had a hand in preparing their attire. The family went to buy materials—cloth for shirts and blouses, skins and feathers for anklets and headdresses. Almost everything has to be made by hand. What the immediate family could not make or buy, they asked friends and relatives to lend them, and through the magic of the pueblo grapevine their needs, and those of all the other families involved in the dance, were met. Everyone is glad to help children who want to dance.

The week before the Feast is a time of intense activity. Food, including dozens of loaves of round oven-bread, must be cooked, and dance clothing is in the final stages of preparation. People are calling on neighbors and friends for last-minute needs—a feather here, a bracelet there. Dance practice is scheduled in the kiva each night.

RAELENE GONZALES, LEFT,
HARVEST DANCE,
SAN ILDEFONSO (SOUTH SIDE)

"DANCING MOCCASINS"
MARY ANSERA, AGE 11
OIL PASTEL

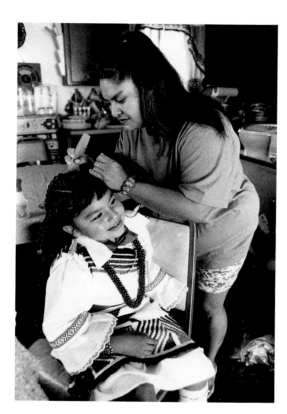

KHAPOVI, AGE 8, AND JUDY HARVIER

"Most everyone gets butterflies at the first practice," Andrew says.

"I wasn't even myself," says Jordan. "I was nervous at the first step and then I can't remember. On the second night I had just a few butterflies, and on the third night, no butterflies!"

"We were all squished up!" exclaims KhaPovi, remembering how it felt to be in a small, windowless space with more than a hundred other people.

The kiva at Santa Clara, built in traditional adobe fashion, has a log-and-bark roof topped with mud. Heavy rains had been falling all week. Water seeped through openings. "It rained during practice and we could feel it inside the kiva," remembers Jordan.

"It's like dancing in a sauna," chuckles Andrew. He adds that the children's practice nights require some sensitive emotional maintenance. "They easily get downcast the first and second nights because they think they don't dance well and they don't know the songs. Songs guide the dance steps. I tell them that I'm learning too and that it gets better, not worse."

"Yeah! On the second night I only made six mistakes," adds Jordan smiling. "I just wanted to keep dancing and not stop until the day came."

And he almost did. "The kids would come back from practice and we'd all be up at my mom's house eating a little something," says Judy. "The boys would put on a tape of the dances and keep dancing until we had to tell them to go to bed."

On the night before the Feast, the Harvier residence on the hill above the pueblo is a beehive of activity. The children have finished their chores—picking weeds and cleaning their rooms—and are playing mini-basketball and Game Boy. Judy is in the kitchen, cooking. At the kitchen table, Andrew works on KhaPovi's tablita, the painted wood headdress that she will wear the next day. Later in the evening KhaPovi, Jordan, and their father attend a final practice in the kiva while Judy works tirelessly preparing food—posole, green chile, red chile, potato salad, and bread pudding.

Jordan returns from the kiva dancing and smiling. KhaPovi enters with eyes beaming bright and unwinds by playing with her brother's Game Boy. Andrew carries in the gear and sighs, "That was a good practice." Taking only a drink of tea, he goes back to work on the tablita. It is 11:30 PM.

The kids are soon sent to bed. Judy and Andrew continue into the early morning working on the dance outfits, preparing food, and completing the endless last-minute, must-do tasks that come from nowhere on such occasions. Sleep is abandoned to the energy of the moment.

FEAST DAY

The next morning, as the first faint rays of sunlight begin to emerge over the mountains, the children are awakened. All the dancers must go to the Rio Grande before dawn to pray and bathe. Some wade, some sprinkle. "I just laid down in it!" exclaims KhaPovi, returning home. "It was cold!"

Getting ready is a family project. Men and boys must dress in the kiva, so Jordan waits while his father begins to wrap buckskin leggings over KhaPovi's moccasins. Uncle Mino arrives to help. Father and son leave. KhaPovi calmly stands in her white cotton tunic while her uncle adjusts her *manta*. Jordan suddenly reappears: "We forgot our rattles!" He's quickly gone. Uncle Mino leaves, too.

Alone now with her mother, KhaPovi sits in the kitchen while Judy binds up her hair. There is only one chance to ensure that hair and headdress will not come loose during a long day of dancing, and that chance is now. KhaPovi fiddles around deciding which earrings to wear. "The watermelon ones or the ones Grandma bought me?"

By 9:30 she is ready to leave. Girls and boys, men and women, all meet in the kiva before the dancing begins. It is time to find your place in line, receive final instructions, and make sure that your outfit is complete.

Dance outfits are elaborate and beautiful. Elders are quick to point out that they are not "costumes," because what happens is not pretend.

KhaPovi wears a white embroidered gown under a hand-woven, embroidered white manta. The manta is belted with a red, black, and green sash and draped with a colorful shawl. For this special occasion, KhaPovi has chosen her mother's wedding shawl. On her feet are deerskin moccasins covered by soft buckskin leggings that are wrapped up to her knees. Tied around her ankles are skunk skins, which are said to protect the dancer's path. Silver bracelets and grandmother's earrings finish the picture. The painted wood headdress will be tied over her thick, braided hair just before the dance.

Jordan wears a richly embroidered, hand-woven dance kilt that was made for his father, over a pair of running shorts. Tucked into the kilt is a white shirt held by a white sash belt and set off by a colored scarf. Today Jordan wears his great-grandpa's beaded moccasins. Skunk skins wrap around the bottom of finely crocheted leggings that run all the way up the leg. Bells at the waist and knees will provide rhythmic accents to the drumming. An elaborate *póhpóvi*, a headdress of parrot, macaw, and eagle feathers, fits snugly on his head. A large gourd rattle filled with small turquoise stones completes Jordan's outfit.

KHAPOVI, AGE 9, AND ANDREW HARVIER

87

Before leaving the kiva, each dancer will receive an evergreen bough and a blessed ear of corn, and will be marked on the cheeks with red clay rouge.

The time to dance draws near. Pueblo residents gather outside. Excitement and anticipation run high. Visitors arrive and may wonder what happens in the kiva before a dance.

"The kiva is our church," says Paul Tsosie, one of the Winter clan drummers, and Jackie's father. "Once the children have made their initiative known, it's up to the rest of us to offer a positive direction and to be examples of how to be respectful. While getting ready for the dance the children gain spiritual development and greater personal responsibility. They become part of a whole and wholesome circle."

What is seen, heard, and shared in the kiva before and during the dances is for participants only. Kiva members are instructed not to share details on the outside. It is

AMO ORTEGA, AGE 12,
KHAPOVI HARVIER, AGE 9,
JORDAN HARVIER, AGE 11,
CORN DANCE,
SANTA CLARA

enough to say that those who don't dance never fully know what it means to be Pueblo.

"We usually offer advice in Tewa," says Paul Tsosie. "There is meditation and a prayer session for those who want to participate."

"One purpose of the kiva is to find out where you're at rather than who you are," suggests Andrew Harvier. "When you're getting ready to dance or practicing in the kiva, it's hot and there's a lot of stress. You see people as they really are. They don't even have to say a thing, and then you see how you fit amongst them as a body."

Watching children dance holds special significance for the community. It means that the culture will be extended and preserved.

"There is gladness and happiness that the children have grown up in such a way that they respect their clan," says Frances Harney, an elementary school teacher who is also participating in the Corn Dance today. "They've been watching for a long time and now want to continue and join with pride. As they come into the kiva and begin to learn, we get a good feeling because we know there will be someone there to take our place should we decide not to dance."

She adds, "We pray by listening to the songs and the beating of the drums. It requires inner listening and feeling. Even if the children don't know their native language, they still communicate through the songs and the dance. The language may fade, but not the dance. We tell the children to ask questions, look at the person across from you, but most importantly, listen to the song."

"And dance hard!" quips Paul Tsosie.

Around eleven o'clock, it is time. The dancers and drummers emerge from the kiva and pause at the top. Slowly, one by one, they descend the wooden stairs. Aglow with pride, KhaPovi walks in front of her father and is helped down the stairs by an elder. The dancers, more than one hundred of them, stand in two parallel lines ready to enter the plaza to the beat of the drum.

And what thoughts go through young dancers' heads when they first come out of the kiva, see hundreds of people watching, climb down the ladder to the plaza, and stand ready to dance?

"The butterflies come back!" exclaims Jordan.

"I get a little shy," says Jackie Tsosie. "I see the people and I think they must be really interested in the dances."

"You feel proud of yourself, like you belong," answers Jordan's cousin Amo Ortega. "I was shaky because a lot of people were there, but you make this effort to dance and you do."

The drummers in the plaza begin, gourd rattles shake, and then they dance! KhaPovi's first steps come as effortlessly as those of the older, more seasoned dancers who surround her. Her father proudly follows her step. Standing in the crowd nearby, Judy is clearly gratified to see her children step in unison to the universal heartbeat for the first time.

This is the Corn Dance. Dancers hold the corn in their right hand and evergreens in their left. "The Corn Dance signifies all crops, especially corn," states Frances Harney. "We use the evergreen because it is like life, it is fresh. It's your life, your breath."

There are usually four cycles of four dances each. Each dance is performed in a separate open area, around which local people set up their chairs, and tourists and non-Indian friends of the pueblo stand. The plaza is full. Between the heads of visitors you see a moving mass of colors—yellow, red, turquoise, brown. The drums, songs, and sounds of the dancers seem to create a song from the Earth herself. The Sun steadily pours down his energy. The Feast lives!

LUNCH BREAK

After two rounds of dancing there is a lunch break. Moccasined women bring trays and baskets of food to the kiva for the boys and men, who must remain there. Meanwhile the girls and women, without their headdresses and covered in their shawls, are allowed to return home to eat. It is a time to gather strength for the afternoon.

Feast means food. Relatives and invited guests gather at homes throughout the pueblo. While some people wait their turn and visit, others are called to the table. "Here's a place for you. Eat! Enjoy!" Mothers and grandmothers serve bowl after colorful bowl of posole, green chile, red chile, garbanzo beans, beef, ham, yellow corn, potato salad, and green salad. Behind the main table may be a counter laden with bread and pies, several varieties of Jell-O salad, and cake. You can wash it all down with generous servings of punch, iced tea, water, or coffee. And no one can leave without a healthy sampling of the very delicious bread pudding.

With bodies replenished and stomachs full, everyone returns to the dance plazas as Santa Clara's Feast Day continues. From atop the Winter clan kiva a few boys and men watch the gathering clouds, waiting for the women and girls to return.

LARISSA AGUILAR

90

"FEAST MEAL"
LARISSA AGUILAR, AGE 5
COLORED PENCIL, OIL PASTEL

DANCING FOR THE PUEBLO

Even though this year's dance is on a weekday, the crowd of spectators has grown. The drummers and dancers emerge and show signs of tiring, especially the children. This is a hot, sweaty business. Neither the approaching dark clouds nor the slight breeze are enough to cool the dancers in their layers of wool and cotton.

Looking out over the plaza pulsating with the movement of dancers and the rhythm of bells, gourd rattles, and drums, it is hard to recognize in these intensely

MICHAEL TAFOYA, CENTER,
COMANCHE DANCE,
SAN JUAN

focused children the squirming, tennis shoe- and T-shirt-clad youngsters who fill the classrooms and playground of the day school, pushing and shoving, chasing and kicking, arguing and laughing, running and teasing. Nevertheless, they are the same kids.

No matter which Pueblo you belong to, there is a special feeling to Feast Day.

"I like to dance because it's fun," states an exuberant Michael Tafoya.

"It helps you out," says Naomi Naranjo. "You feel special 'cause you're dancing."

"I like Feast 'cause we wear all kinds of things that are *real* nice," say Angela and Christine Pacheco together.

"What do I like about dancing?" asks Audrey Lujan. "Well, you can see all your friends, and you can communicate with the elders," she says slowly, enunciating each syllable. She laughs, but I hear a note of respect in her voice.

"You go to practice and all your friends are there," adds Julie Vigil. "I wore out two holes in my mocs."

JOSEPH CHAVARRIA,
HARVEST DANCE,
SANTA CLARA

"I like dancing and food, food, food, food!" exclaims Devonna Naranjo. "It's hard work, too. It makes you sleep good. We dance so we can remember what people celebrated a long time ago."

"Well, there's good reasons and bad reasons to dance at Feast," begins Daniel Archuleta, as though delivering a lecture. "The good reason is you're dancing for the pueblo and one of the bad reasons is those tourist ladies looking at you." He furrows his brow and opens his mouth in imitation of someone gawking.

"EAGLE DANCER"
DANIEL ARCHULETA, AGE 10
94   TEMPERA

"You have to be powerful—not powerful, what is that word? I forgot," adds Tricia Dasheno. "And you have to think your best about it. You have to pray when you're in the kiva and you have to dance the best that you can."

Many of the children are experienced dancers who clearly recall the first time they danced.

"I was supposed to go to the right and instead I went to the left by myself!" Mauricia Chavarria says with a laugh. "I think I was four and a half."

"I started dancing when I was three," says Jerome Tafoya. "Every time we have a dance I go. For our Harvest Dance you get to wear the gray mud paint. It makes you feel warm, like you're in the sun swimming."

"It was when I was six or five or maybe older," recalls Naomi. "I didn't dance the whole way. I guess I was dancing and nodding off, so my grandpa came and got me and took me to my grandma's house. She let me fall asleep. After lunch I woke up and wanted to dance, so they put me back in."

"The first time I danced was the Green Corn," says Pam Cata. "I have a picture in my house. I have a mushroom-head hair-do! I didn't want to dance but these people came from France and they already asked my mom if they could take a picture of me so I had to dance."

"I first danced at San I when I was really small. I was just sitting in the middle of the circle crying," Lydia Martinez recalls with a grin. "It was the Comanche Dance and I was scared. Those guys took me to my grandma Siri's." Lydia is referring to the men and older boys who act as guards at every dance. They pick up feathers, evergreen boughs, bells, and other parts of dance outfits that may fall off during the dance. They also sell photo passes when photography is permitted, keep the spectators from bothering the dancers and drummers, and take care of any dancers having trouble completing the dance.

"I had to stand in front with the leaders so I could learn how, 'cause I'd done real bad at practice," Devonna tells me. "The people got mad at me 'cause I did it wrong. Then they showed me how to do it right and put me up front, with the loud noises. *Bom, bom, bom, bom.* It feels like you're getting hit on the head with a hammer. I only danced half the day. I was tiny. I was six years old. I tried to relax myself so I wouldn't get scared."

"I was two years old when I first danced," says Katie. "It was the Comanche Dance. The whole family danced. I was scared, but I was ready."

"THE SINGING DRUM"
JACKIE TSOSIE, AGE 10
TEMPERA

"I was three years old when I first started dancing," remembers Jackie Lopez. "By lunch time I started getting tired and then I started crying. My uncle took me home and I got to eat," she adds with a chuckle.

"And I got stuck dancing all day and didn't even know she left," adds her mother, Patricia. "When we broke for lunch I couldn't find her." Mother and daughter laugh together now, but Jackie says she wasn't laughing then. "It was really hot," says Patricia.

"And all the stuff they make you wear," adds Jackie.

"And she still hasn't finished a dance," exclaims her mom with a laugh. They argue a little.

Months later, after she has read the rough draft of this book, Jackie writes me a note: "And Bruce, I *did* finish the dance this year!"

ENDING THE DAY

Now the third dance set is over, and the dancers return to the kiva as they have done between all the sets. It's after five o'clock, and most visitors have left.

A thunderclap, followed by a short but steady downpour, accompanies the start of the last set of dances. The children exult in the rain with joyful laughter. Grandmothers on the sidelines nod knowingly, as if they knew all along that the dance would bring rain.

The brief shower passes and the dance continues. As the dancers enter the long second plaza, a rainbow appears over them. The air tingles with new rain and silent rejoicing. There is a renewed sense of spirit and energy in each dancer's step. Yawns and half-closed eyes are replaced by bright smiles. The dancers have brought the rainbow!

To be at a dance is to participate. You bring your good thoughts and send them out to the dancers and the whole world. Your input is as essential as the dancing and drumming, and will be returned to you a thousandfold. Pueblo dances honor the people's connection to land and spirit. They therefore honor all of life—including tourists!

It is time to finish. Each dance group conducts the last dance in front of its own kiva. Slowly, to the cadence of the drummers standing near the kiva steps, the dancers enter the plaza through a narrow alley. The atmosphere is charged with anticipation and emotion. To show their appreciation, the clan families conduct a giveaway, bestowing gifts on the dancers and tossing fruit and trinkets into the crowd.

Family members now enter the dance, crowding the dance space and erasing the line between spectator and participant. The drums and songs swell and reverberate off every surface. The sound is taken in and becomes heart. Dancers' feet come within inches of mine. As I crouch near the ground, a few boys I know shake their rattles very close to my head, smiling.

The drums beat louder as the dancers mount the kiva stairs. When the last dancer has climbed the ladder, the drummers end their song with a gesture to the crowd. Bringing their drumsticks and evergreen boughs to their mouths, they breathe in, and then extend them out to the crowd as they say in the Tewa language, "May you all have a good, long life." The crowd responds with the same words, and then all is quiet. A natural single breath comes from and flows over everyone present. The moment is temporarily suspended. All are one.

The crowd slowly disperses. Friends are greeted. Tewa language flows freely. Kids playing tag run between the legs of adults. There is laughter as family members wait for their dancers.

And inside the kiva . . . That's secret, remember?

Judy Harvier waits outside the kiva for KhaPovi, Jordan, and Andrew to emerge. Then they all go to the river together to make quiet prayers and to spread cornmeal on the flowing waters.

Back at home, KhaPovi first seeks out her cat, Shadow, and cuddles it close to her manta. Judy has set another feast on the table and guests begin to arrive. Then KhaPovi and Jordan turn to their usual evening activities—coloring books, TV—while they snack on candy they received during the give-aways. Neither of them appears tired.

I ask them, "What is the dance about?"

"The corn is like a blessing," says Jordan immediately, with a look that says he has surprised himself with his answer. "A friend can come get it from you to use as decoration in their house or eat it."

". . . or replant it," adds his father quietly. "It's a cycle."

"It's to plant it, to cook it, and to make the corn grow," interjects KhaPovi. But how does a dance make corn grow?

"I keep thinking that dancers are corn and they grow," KhaPovi tells me. "The song sings to the corn. I think maybe the song talks to the corn, saying, 'Will you grow?'"

I am reminded of that old adage about wisdom coming from the mouths of children. There may be adults who have not figured out what this girl already knows.

JOSHUA POVIJUA, PAINTING HIMSELF
AS A BUFFALO DANCER

97

"How did you learn to dance?" Andrew asks his children.

"Practice? Watching the others?" Both answers are questions, searching.

"Did someone tell you what to do with your feet?" asks Andrew. "Did they say, 'Do this, do that,' or did you read an instruction manual?"

There is laughter as KhaPovi fidgets. Then she says, clearly and distinctly, "I listened to me."

Indeed, the children learn by listening and observing. Through drum, song, and the good feeling of the community, the dance is drawn out of them, naturally, because it's always been there. It has been passed down to them for thousands of years and now dwells in them forever.

After dinner KhaPovi sinks into the sofa and plays with her brother's portable video game. Her turquoise and coral beads are reflected on the animated screen of a far different world. A quiet smile graces her face.

A Pueblo child's first dance steps mark the beginning of her introduction to the heart of Pueblo culture. In the dance you commune with friends, family, and elders while contributing to the overall well-being of the entire Pueblo. Once you are in line, once the drum is beating, there is little time for butterflies. The music envelops you and you begin to move to the rhythm of life.

May your life be long!

LEE MOQUINO (WITH RED FLAG),
COMANCHE DANCE,
SAN ILDEFONSO (SOUTH SIDE)

"PUEBLO PLAZA"
JUAN DE LA CRUZ, AGE 12
PEN AND INK

No Matter Who You Are,
You Belong to the Earth

JUAN DE LA CRUZ

JUAN DE LA CRUZ GAZES UP at the underbelly of a model B-17 bomber suspended from a viga, one of the round wooden beams that support the roof of his bedroom. An F-16 model hangs from the next beam over. The walls of the room are decorated with favorite movie posters and a wide array of Juan's academic and art awards. Board games, books, shoes, and the accumulated toys of youth line the shelves. This twelve-year-old's room is not very different from that of any other child his age. In many ways, Juan is a regular kid.

"I play video games," says Juan. "I like to work on models, draw, or just go outside and play and climb around. I go down into that big old trench and bust bottles with a metal pole. I go down there to kill time. Actually I have a good time doing it, breaking bottles."

Juan is an advanced student, a natural-born artist, a consummate sketcher. He can make front, side, and three-quarter views of any subject and knows how to use shading and depth with the maturity of a trained adult. One of his drawings, a figure from the movie *Stargate*, hangs in the kitchen. Juan's mother, Loec, tells me that Juan made the drawing by starting at the bottom of the paper and working up: "He ran out of paper and we had to tape another one on so he could finish," she says. The drawing exhibits perfect proportion and an incredible amount of shaded detail. I wonder aloud where his talent comes from, and Loec recalls that when Juan was an infant his father lined his hospital room bassinet with pictures of paintings that he had cut out from magazines.

101

"FUNNY FOOTBALL PLAYERS"
JEFF MARTINEZ, AGE 8
WATERCOLOR

"Derek didn't see why Juan should have to look at white walls," Loec says. "The nurse came in and questioned what he was doing, but then she noticed how Juan was focusing on the pictures. It was like we had discovered something."

SOURCES OF INSPIRATION

All good artists find subject matter in their immediate surroundings. At the turn of the century young Tewa artists, many of whom were taught and encouraged by Anglo patrons, primarily depicted dances and traditional Pueblo designs. Today, however, the visual climate that attracts a Pueblo child's attention is much more diverse. She is as likely to draw a video game warrior, a rainbow, or a low-rider car as a kiva or a Pueblo design.

"Because he's tough," says Naomi Naranjo, explaining why she chose to draw a portrait of NBA star Charles Barkley.

"I like to draw cars," says Nolan Cruz. "I used to draw Ninja Turtles."

NFL team insignias (especially the Dallas Cowboys and Denver Broncos), cartoon and animated movie characters, and current pop cultural icons—these are the images on the minds of Pueblo children today. And why not? Children across the country are more alike than different. Since they share the same culture, thanks to television and the other media, it should come as no surprise that they share similar imagery.

"I like drawing people," says Devonna Naranjo. "Not the standard princesses, but pretty much regular people."

Justin Dasheno says, "I draw animals, monsters, dogs, sometimes people, cars, and games like Game Gear."

"Hands, trees, clowns, and my sister," adds Larissa Aguilar. "That's all!"

JAMES MARTINEZ, NOLAN CRUZ, KEVIN AGUINO

LARISSA AGUILAR

It is important that children have the opportunity to recognize and express the whole of who they are. To limit Pueblo children to drawing only Indian designs would be like allowing people of English descent to perform only Morris dancing. Such an attitude is ultimately patronizing; besides, the children would never stand for it. When youngsters are encouraged to explore a variety of art forms and expressions, their own culture takes on greater personal value.

"Well, the first subject is the eagle," explains Daniel Archuleta. "Then there's pottery, faces, dogs . . . dead dogs! I like to draw balloons, the ones that people go up in. I draw this house, whatever is on the TV, my room, and those fish." He gestures around the room.

"I cannot draw animals and I cannot draw people," says Julie Vigil emphatically. "Except sometimes we draw people we don't like and make them look very awful. We laugh at them. And I don't like drawing pictures about New Mexico either. I don't like always having to draw yucca and mountains and all that."

Julie's comments evince an adult maturity and bring up a matter connected to being part of a minority culture. Some people believe art by Indian children should be totally Indian in motif. The children reject attempts to stereotype them, insisting on their individuality.

"Are you proud of your Pueblo culture? Do you dance at Feast? Can you draw me some Indian designs? What's it like to be a Pueblo?" Julie mimics the typical tourist's questions, rolling her bright brown eyes. Like the other children, she knows about being stereotyped. "We're proud of what we are, but we are people first, *then* Native American," she adds pointedly.

DOING THINGS

Children are basically mobile and verbal. Their primary art forms are playing, teasing, running, and talking. The complaint "There's nothing to do" is not heard often here in the pueblos. How do the children spend their time?

"Well, first of all, I like to play basketball, draw, watch TV, listen to the radio, or just talk to myself, saying things like, 'I wish I was 18 so I could drive the car,'" says Daniel, with dreams in his eyes. "I sit here and watch TV and think to myself. My favorite shows are *Family Matters, Full House, Roseanne, Coach, Batman, Fox Kids Club Funhouse, The Tiny Tunes.* One more, one more. That science guy."

"THE TWO PANDAS"
POVI HERRERA, AGE 5
MARKER, OIL PASTEL, WATERCOLOR

"I watch TV and play tag," laughs Larissa. "I tag my own self!"

"I listen to the radio and play outside," says her sister Elena.

"I play Chinese jump rope and climb in my tree house," says Nathana Bird. "I have little plastic pots and I play house. I go in the dog's pen and the dog chases me so I get out. I sometimes go to my little steep hill and jump down. I made little stairs to get back up."

"I like to draw, play basketball outside, listen to my radio, and go to my friend's or my cousin's house," replies Nolan Cruz. Nolan's mother, Patricia, recalls a time when children's play was a little different.

"When I was little there was a whole bunch of us kids running around the pueblo," she says. "It was so much fun! And we didn't have to have toys, we played with what we could find, cans, sticks, rocks, climbing trees. We weren't supposed to climb on top of the houses, but, you know, kids are kids, we didn't pay attention, so we went and climbed on top of the houses, we jumped from the houses, things like that. Now the kids have to have toys to play with. But that's how I grew up. I tell Nolan stories like that, and every once in a while he'll say, 'Mom, you know what? I wish I could have been little with you and we could have played games together.'" Childhood is a magic time whose experience links children of all ages together.

KELLY GIBSON, JASMINE CASAVAS, ARIA SANDERS, ROCHELLE NARANJO

Jerome Tafoya and I are riding our bikes. He's the kind of kid I'd want to play with a lot if we were the same age. Smart and polite, he's full of stories in which there is a fine line between fact and fiction.

"I like to go to the river and ride my bike all over the place," Jerome says. "I go down to the corrals and make a fire, eat some marshmallows, kill a robin and then eat its heart, and then go hunting again. They're little ones like that," he says, closing his fingers to the size of an M&M. "When you take out the heart it tastes like *bunse* [bread pudding]. If you add a little bit of salt it tastes like pork chops."

I look at him incredulously. "Really?"

"Yeah! They're good."

"Do you cook them?" I inquire.

"Nope!" he says, and breaks into a teasing smile.

"Right after school I eat and watch *Saved by the Bell*," says a very businesslike Devonna. "Then if it's Wednesday I go to my dad's until the next day. We're usually at his friend's house, somewhere eating, or on our way to a basketball game. And oh yeah, homework. I try to scrunch that in a bit. Then if I'm not with my dad I stay home, not rushing. In the summer when my mom's at work I go to my grandma's house and make messes, like digging and stuff, being bad. My mom doesn't know that. And you better not tell her, either!"

"Sometimes I do nothing. Nothing is just sitting around watching TV," says Naomi. "When I'm doing that I get ideas. I'll be checking channels and they'll be doing something educational. I'll say 'Oh! I want to try that!' So I'll get out the stuff that I need and try it."

"I walk home to my grandma's every day and start doing my homework," says Justin. "When I finish I have the rest of my time to play baseball in the yard, meet the neighbors, eat, watch TV, and play Supernintendo. Sometimes on Saturdays I watch *X-Men* and then I call my cousin and we play. On Sunday we go to church and visit our relatives. I ride my bike to see my auntie, and sometimes I ride to the river to see if there are ducks. There's these big hills and when it snows we go sledding."

"I come home, do my homework, play a little bit, and then run back to school because I forgot some of my homework," says Tricia Dasheno with a laugh. "On weekends I play with my friends, run up the hills with my dogs, put my sister on my bike and push her off and make her cry. Yeah, I do."

"She's a crazy lady," affirms her cousin Justin.

"I sit in my truck or in the tree and talk to myself," says Pam Cata. "I watch cars pass by and run from my dog."

"We just talk about people," says Lydia Martinez. "Well, not people but b-o-y-s! And we do all kinds of crazy stuff."

"She's dangerous," adds her best friend, Pam.

"Yeah, I'm dangerous," Lydia agrees, nodding her head. "I sit in the middle of the road and we talk, a car comes . . . and . . . we just stay there. I climb trees. I climb to the tops. I also bother everybody's stuff. I read my sister's letters. She'll kill me if she finds out."

NOLAN CRUZ

NOLAN'S NATURE WALK

Nolan Cruz hides in the kitchen when I first come in. He is soon discovered and we discuss what photographs to make to show who he is and what he does. As we move toward the back door, Nolan's aunt teases him: "He spends longer than a girl fixing his hair every day! Photograph him doing that!" Twelve-year-old Nolan smiles quietly and runs his hand through his black, slicked-backed hair.

The field behind the house is covered in chain cholla, a large and wiry form of cactus. "Do you ever go there?"

"Yeah. We kinda go on a nature walk, like scientific." Nolan sets off down a long, narrow dirt trail. Two of his friends and I follow. "There's one place where there's lots of rabbits, another where we break bottles, and another, well, you'll see . . ."

107

"LOVE STORY"
JAKE NARANJO, AGE 11
COLORED PENCIL

Nolan and his friends walk ahead of me, talking quietly. Occasionally they look back and smile as we cross a dry section of desert punctuated by tatters of plastic refuse, cans, and bottles. I can't imagine any rabbits living here. The boys are soon darting under cholla to grab bottles. One is tossed on the ground and another quickly thrown at it, breaking both. I glance up at Nolan with a "You call this entertainment?" look on my face. His eyebrows raise, a smile forms, and he exclaims, "The sound!"

One of the boys suggests we search for "painted sticks." "They're over by that hole, where the land goes down," he says. Soon we're in an arroyo. "Here's one, Bruce!" exclaims Nolan. He points to a short gray stick lying on the ground. It's about the size of a pencil, dried and weathered. At first it looks completely natural. A closer look reveals tiny cotton cords tied to the stick, and a faint trace of paint. Curious, I reach to pick it up. "Don't touch it!" warns Nolan with a parent's sternness.

"Here's another one!" shouts one of the boys. A small feather, its end wrapped in twine, is tied to a rabbit brush. "There's lots of them around here usually," says Nolan. "Sometimes they're painted, but I think these are older 'cause the paint is gone."

"What do you suppose . . . ," I begin.

"I don't know," says Nolan quickly, cutting in. His eyes and those of the boys tell me they have a few ideas. I know about Hopi *pahos*, prayer bundles of painted sticks and feathers offered to the katsinas. The Hopi and Tewa people share similar ceremonies. Perhaps the sticks are evidence of Pueblo "doings," I suggest. Shoulders shrug. No one speaks. I perceive a nervous silence born of not quite knowing what to say about something that may be a cultural secret. Maybe it's better to leave things alone, to acknowledge that the land holds mysteries. We turn around and race home.

OUTSIDE AND IN

These children have a natural affinity with the out-of-doors. It is their home, their playground, and they spend a great deal of time there.

"We go outside mostly every, every, every, every single day," sing Angela and Christine Pacheco in unison. "Sometimes we go to the river with our brother or sister."

The world is made of stories, and stories make experience. The children commune with nature through their stories.

"I go to the canyon with my dad to go fishing," says Devonna. "Squirrels once came to our camp and ate all our food, all my chips. There was a storm and we were in the van. Somebody left them out there and we watched the squirrels eat all the chips. It was their Feast Day!"

"Every time snow falls, if it's that good type you can pack, I make an attack on my dad with a snowball," recounts Juan with glee. "A couple of days ago, before the snow melted away, I kept on blasting him with snowballs down at the barn when he was chopping wood. He told me that after he was done chopping wood he'd rub my face in snow. I thought he was bluffing, but he did it!"

"Once in a while, if it's nice, I go outside and ride bikes with my friends," says Julie. "In the summer it's often very hot so I stay inside with the air conditioning, and there's nothing to do outside anyhow. You should enjoy nature now while you have it, but I don't," she states bluntly. "Instead I watch TV every single day for maybe three hours."

Contemporary media, especially television and home videos, have had a dramatic impact on young people of all cultures. It is easy to cast them as the villains in the ongoing process of cultural change. But have they replaced traditional storytellers or merely become the new storytellers?

Much of what is true and powerful in traditional culture has great difficulty competing with the quick pace and dramatic, often violent action found on television and in movies. Stories are quiet and require active listening; TV, in comparison, is passive. Often it will be turned on but not listened to. Yet it is the same kids who race home to watch the *Power Rangers*, MTV, or *Saved by the Bell* who dance the Deer, the Comanche, and the Corn. Clearly, a new balance is being struck.

"When I get up in the morning and get ready for school I'll watch TV for a little while," says Shanna Naranjo. "And then when I come home from school I watch some more. We watch TV during dinner, and on weekends I watch TV a lot, mostly movies. But I go outside about fifty times a week."

"I go outside every day and watch TV every day for two or three hours," Jackie Lopez tells me. "My mom says I'd better not watch too much or I'll turn into a couch potato!"

ARIA SANDERS, WITH ART
THAT SHE PRODUCED AT HOME

HOME LIFE

If you were to peek inside the home lives of Pueblo children, you'd probably find they are not too different from your own. There are chores and homework to be done. Children are expected to do their fair share to support the family.

"I take out the trash. Sometimes I have to do the dishes. I sweep, mop, sometimes vacuum, clean my room, help cook, and that's about it," states Nolan.

"I *should* clean my room. I'm told to clean my room, but I don't," says Julie.

"I make my bed. I wash the windows and sometimes I'll cook dinner," offers Shanna. "I make spaghetti, French toast, lasagna, and I can make really good-tasting salads."

"Chores?" says Naomi. "Mine are keeping my dog fed, the chickens, my horse, the other horses. We have twenty-something cows and four horses. I do the towels, wash dishes, trash, normal stuff like that, keep my room clean."

"I have to pick up the trash and throw it in the dumpster," states Jerome. "Then I have to scrub the toilet," he adds with an embarrassed smile.

"We clean the house!" shout Angela and Christine together, looking at each other and laughing.

Pueblo families are like those found in communities all over the world. They are loving, caring, supportive, and generous. Some are dysfunctional. There are troubled families, single-parent families, and divided families. In many homes parents and children are the best of friends. Cousins, aunts, uncles, and grandparents are people you spend a lot of time with. They are your neighbors and comrades. Culture-related and other activities serve to bind families together.

"To me, my family is the best friend I ever had," says KhaPovi Harvier, gesturing with two thumbs up like movie critics Siskel and Ebert. "I can talk to them, tease them, watch TV with them, and play games with them."

"Everybody is always busy so we never have free time for ourselves except on weekends," says Mauricia Chavarria. "On weekdays we're busy from 6:30 in the morning to 10:30 at night, and on the weekends we go to Albuquerque and spend the day together. We shop."

"We eat together and watch TV together. We talk on the phone together," says Nathana. "We wash dishes together. We laugh together over a little joke."

"Sometimes we play games together," reports Michael Tafoya. "We talk about what's going on with the pueblo, what's going on at the gym, what's going on at school, what's going on in the neighborhood, and how much money of Mom's we have to spend."

"We eat!" shouts a sibling from another room, and everyone laughs.

"My dad always takes us on a ride or to the mountains and tells us stories about when my mom and he were dating," Naomi says. "Most of the time we go to the mall or out to eat. My dad is real energetic. He doesn't want to stay in one place. So sometimes we go with him because he takes us places. We'll go feed the cows and he'll be driving all over everywhere. It's fun!"

"We go to the canyon and fish all day and maybe camp out," says Jerome. "Sometimes we take a walk down to the river. At home we watch movies and eat dinner together. We listen to country music and exercise together. We talk and tell stories."

PERCEPTIONS AND THE REAL THING

Each year thousands of people visit the pueblos, seeking a glimpse of what it is to be Indian in this day and age. Some are merely curious, some have done extensive reading, and still others are there to see how much Indian life today resembles the way it is represented in the media.

"Probably the first thing they do is look to see if we're wearing rags," says Juan, "since that's what the pictures in history books usually show." Juan is referring to depictions of the ancient Anasazi unclothed or dressed in animal skins.

"Indians in the movies are always in feathers and they don't have many clothes on. When people come here they look at you all weird 'cause you're just in regular clothes like they are," says Heather Dasheno.

"Most of the tourists that I've met seem like they're amazed," says Shanna. "They'll say, 'Is it like living somewhere else?' And I'll say, 'I don't know. I've never lived anywhere else!'"

"They ask you the dumbest questions that you'll ever hear!" exclaims Lydia. "They should figure out what it is, like charades. Or they should just watch. They don't need to know all that stuff to appreciate us."

Pueblo children and adults alike find themselves bombarded with questions. Dealing with curious and well-intentioned visitor questions can be a test of patience. Each visitor asks a question only once, but residents must answer repeatedly. There are also times, especially during a dance, when *any* talk borders on rudeness.

"I was at my grandma's house with my cousin when a whole busload of tourists came up to us," recalls Naomi. "They go, 'Oh! So cute! Can we take your picture?' We looked at each other like . . . ," Naomi rolls her eyes and raises her eyebrows, "and then we asked them, 'Why?' My grandma quickly said, 'Don't say that. That's disrespectful.' They said

"TWO INDIAN TRAVELERS"
JAMES ROMERO, AGE 10
TEMPERA

they wanted to show people back home what Indians looked like. We were in our regular, everyday clothes, and we looked at each other after they left and wondered how come. We don't look different than anybody else."

Angela has a similar sentiment. "I think people should mind their own business and not worry about us. We don't live in teepees and we only wear feathers in our hair when we're dancing. We live in a house and have a clean floor, not mud!"

Many Pueblo kids correspond with pen pals who ask them about being Indian. The exercise of answering can become irksome.

"My pen pal asked me if I was part Cherokee, and if I lived in a teepee, and if I traded with the settlers, and if my Indian name was Pocahontas!" laughs Mauricia. "And she asked me if I've ever seen any kind of clothes, famous clothes like Bongo, Union Bay, things like that. And she asked me if the boys still wear a G-string."

"It makes us feel real stupid," states her sister, Danielle, "and I think *they're* stupid, because it's the real world now."

Feelings are easily hurt when a well-intentioned letter or visitor's comment focuses only on what is stereotypically Indian. The children have heard it over and over again. They desire only to be respected as people, as individuals. And they have advice for readers and visitors.

"Well, the first thing is that it's not how it's usually mentioned in books or TV," says Naomi. "We're modern people. We don't do anything different but our Indian ways. So when you come it'll be just like any other place. On a regular working day not many people will be around, just probably some kids, some people driving around, and busses dropping off kids."

"It doesn't matter what race you are," says Mauricia. "No matter who you are, you belong to the Earth, and there's nothing that can ever change that because the Earth is your mother." Then she adds with a grin, "Your turn, Bob!"

"Live in the now!" stresses Devonna. "What I mean is, we live the same as you do. We dress the same as you do. We're the same as you. We're just regular kids!"

"And we're not just anybody," sing Pam and Lydia together. "We're special. Believe us. It's true!"

"LADY IN THE BLUE DRESS"
ROSE BEAN, AGE 12
OIL PASTEL

Thoughts on a Bean Pot

AN AFTERWORD

JUAN DE LA CRUZ AND I HAVE MOVED into a small room of his parents' cozy, wood-stove-heated home near the middle of Santa Clara Pueblo. On his computer screen Juan examines a moving graphic of a warplane. He is looking for the enemy, Baron von Something-or-other. Atop the adjacent hard drive, pairs of plastic Power Ranger figures stand neatly in a line. Outside, where the sky shows its last winter light, it is clear and cold.

Inside, however, it is warm and busy. Juan's slender fingers dance over the keyboard, striking keys that cause the plane to spin and shoot, speed up and dive. As he works Juan explains the game to me, at a level of computer detail well beyond my capacity to understand.

Above the ceiling vigas lie layers of wood and then dirt. Juan, with his dreams of flying B-17 bombers, may live in the most traditional home in the pueblo. Except for a small heater in his parents' bedroom, all heating and cooking are done with wood.

The family's self-described "Walton's Mountain" philosophy may be one key to maintaining culture, for it demands a radically different lifestyle from that found in the outside world. When I ask how he will keep Juan in touch with his past while preparing him for the future, Juan's good-humored father, Derek, quietly gets up from the wooden table and walks into the kitchen. He returns holding two clay pots, which he sets down in front of me. One is darkly stained and has a piece missing from the rim. The other is wonderfully shaped, with a lid and two small handles on opposite sides. Dark fire stains wave up from the bottom. Both are micaceous bean pots, well used.

"You might say that these are our family values," says Derek softly. "The chipped pot belonged to Juan's great-grandmother. There's no telling how many pots of beans it has cooked. The other pot is the one we use. To me the bean pot is symbolic of how we want to and should live life. It looks simple but there is a lot connected to it. For starters, Loec"— Juan's mother—"made this pot with her own hands, from clay she gathered and prepared, for us to use in cooking our family's food. We cook on a wood stove and so I must have plenty of wood ready. That means chopping, learning to use the ax properly, and gathering the wood from the canyon. The rhythm of our life is determined by these simple things. We hope that Juan will one day know these things."

Right now that possibility entails a real leap of faith. Juan is in the living room watching television. Rather than sitting quietly he is engaging the TV, reacting to the action, faking getting shot as he lurches towards the couch, making sounds of gun and laser warfare, fighting back.

Later, as I drive away, I find myself wondering if Juan will take one of those bean pots with him when he goes away to college. My hope for him, and for all the children, is that a bean pot will be their co-pilot in life.

Bruce Hucko

Acknowledgments

"BUFFALO SHIELD"
NOLAN CRUZ, AGE 12
WATERCOLOR

THE INITIAL INSPIRATION FOR THIS BOOK came from the first children I befriended: KhaPovi and Jordan, Nicole and Kim, Naomi and Sarah, Kevin, and Starr. The years spent working in the Pueblo communities were energized by Eliza, Rose, Angela and Christine, Natalie, Joshua, Justin, Raelene, Mark, and Luciano, and by Aria's hugs and Kasia's smile. The project was completed with the persistence and creative companionship of Jackie L., Jackie T., Jerome, Lee, Lydia, Daniel, Devonna, and Dayna.

To all of the Pueblo children I have worked with, I say *"Kúdaawóháa."* Whether or not your photograph, painting, or words appear here, you should know that this is *your* book. These pages are merely notes on the marvelous experience of working with you over the years. In my mind each one of you is part of this work, just as all of you are part of my heart.

These children come to us from wonderful parents and other relatives, several of whom are quoted in the text. For their friendship, trust, and guidance I thank Evelyn Aguilar, Patricia Cruz, Loec and Derek De La Cruz, Frances Harney, Linda and Dale Martinez, Laurie and Louis Naranjo, Mary Naranjo, Tessie Naranjo, Theresa Naranjo, Nora Naranjo-Morse, Shirley and Manuel Pacheco, Bernadette Sanders, Roxanne Swentzell, and Dorothy and Paul Tsosie. I extend heartfelt appreciation to Judy and Andrew Harvier, who invited me into their home and family and whose thoughts, friendship, and spirit provided me with creative sustenance and much-needed roots.

This work would not have been possible without the support of the schools. The staff and principals of the Pueblo day schools are a model of devotion to education. To each of you, the school boards, and the Eight Northern Indian Pueblos Agency Office of Education, I say that it is a privilege to serve with you in the education of the children.

As we go through life we all meet people who help guide us. It may be through a thought, a book, a long friendship, or a chance encounter; whatever the occasion, the gift helps us along our way. My life of working with children, especially Pueblo children, was prompted and supported by Susan Beck, the children of Montezuma Creek, Utah, the Utah Arts Council, Sue Heath, Terry Tempest Williams, the Rockefeller Brothers Fund, J. Edson Way, Celia Calloway, Dollie Naranjo, Larry Littlebird, and the writing of Robert Coles. Special thanks go to Frontier Frames of Santa Fe for supplying us with mat boards over the years.

The School of American Research Press had the vision to support the concept of a book created with the Pueblo community. I thank Joan O'Donnell, director of publications, for her insight, direction, and faith in the project. Editor Jo Ann Baldinger transformed the manuscript into a graceful text and in the process taught me respect for her craft; art director Deborah Flynn Post involved the children in her own creative process to produce an appealing book design that presents all participants well; and publications project coordinator Baylor Chapman cheerfully kept us all together and on schedule.

Thanks go as well to the Annenberg Foundation, which supported the project through the SAR 1995 Task Force on Educational Enrichment, and to the Santa Fe teachers who participated in a stimulating dialogue about the development and potential classroom uses of the book. I also thank Samuel B. Ballen and Bill Cowles for their enthusiastic and generous support of the project.

This book could not have been completed without the love of my parents, Jeanne and Steve Hucko, and Becky Knouff.

Lastly, I acknowledge the spirit of land, community, and creativity that unites us all. If this book leads you to regard the lives of Pueblo children, as well as your own life, home, and creativity, with greater respect, then it has accomplished its task.

A NOTE ON THE VOICES

The voices presented here come from four of the six Tewa-speaking pueblos. An individual may live at one pueblo, be an enrolled member of another, and dance at several others. Most of the children are also linked by family to several pueblos. It would be cumbersome to enumerate all the communities they "belong" to. We have therefore chosen not to list each child's pueblo associations. Their relatives know who they are, and that is what counts. The children speak as individuals, but their combined voices constitute a unified community whose creative spirit erases boundaries set by politics and other outside forces.

Index to the Illustrations

Page numbers in boldface refer to artwork; others indicate photographs.